COVENANT BLESSINGS

Timeless Promises & Inspiring Insights

by
Rod Parsley

Unless otherwise indicated, all Scripture quotations are taken from the *King James Version* of the Bible.

Scriptures taken from THE MESSAGE BIBLE, NEW TESTAMENT WITH PSALMS AND PROVERBS. © 1993, 1994, 1995 by Eugene H. Peterson. Used by permission.

ISBN: 1-880244-40-3
Copyright © 1997 by Rod Parsley.

Published by:
Results Publishing
Box 32903
Columbus, Ohio 43232-0903 USA

Table of Contents

Covenant Blessings for Equipping the Saints

Covenant Blessings for You and Your Family

Covenant Blessings of God's Provision

Covenant Blessings When Facing Life's Storms

Covenant Blessings In Times of . . .

Covenant Blessings for God's Guidance

Covenant Blessings for Your Christian Walk

Covenant Blessings of God's Promises

Covenant Blessings for the Virtuous Christian

Covenant Blessings of Heaven

ROD PARSLEY CELEBRATING

REPAIRING THE BREACH • RAISING THE STANDARD

• REAPING THE HARVEST •

20th ANNIVERSARY

A Word About
Covenant

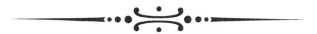

Since the beginning of time in the elegant Garden of Eden, God has established covenants with His choicest servants.

Throughout the pages of history, among saints and sinners alike, covenants have been common among all nations and people.

What exactly is a covenant?

A covenant is an agreement or contract, if you will, between two parties. It is usually made for three specific reasons—protection, business and love.

The ritual for making a covenant usually involved the slaying of innocent animals and the pronouncement of blessings and cursings between the participants of the covenant.

Abraham, the friend of God, was the first man with whom God made a covenant. Proclamation was made and the divine decree was set when, from the lips of the eternal Creator came these words:

And I will bless thee, and make thy name great and thou shalt be a blessing: And I will bless them that bless thee, and curse him that curseth thee: and in thee shall all families of the earth be blessed (Genesis 12:2-3).

This covenant, however, could only offer a temporary solution to an eternal problem—sin. Atonement was a yearly ritual to cover, not remove, the sins of individuals and nations.

So God sent His Son, our Canaan King, Jesus, to offer an eternal propitiation for sin-infected humanity. Hebrews chapter 8, verses 6 and 7 declare:

But now hath he obtained a more excellent ministry, by how much also he is the mediator of a better covenant, which was established upon better promises. For if that first covenant had been faultless, then should no place have been sought for the second.

It is because of this new and better covenant that you and I have not only the privilege but also the right to all the covenant blessings promised throughout the Bible.

As I sat down to write this book, I thought of you, my Covenant Partner, and our precious covenant. I treasure our relationship and do not take lightly the commitment you have made to stand, pray and believe with Joni, with me and this ministry.

Therefore, out of my deepest appreciation and love for you I have produced this special, 20th Anniversary Commerative edition book, *Covenant Blessings*.

In this book I have delved through the pages of the Bible to share with you the covenant blessings, of God's infallible Word— which I trust for every situation of my life and ministry. I have also included insights and revelation that the Holy Spirit has given me over the years concerning each of these covenant blessings.

It is my prayer that, as you meditate and open your spirit to the truths revealed throughout these pages, the Lord will ignite in your spirit the very revelation you need to encourage and inspire you in your daily walk with Him.

Thank you for being my Covenant Partner. Joni and I pray for you daily and believe the abundant blessings of God will manifest in every area of your life. We love you and appreciate you so very much. God bless you!

Your Covenant Partner,

Rod Parsley

ROD PARSLEY CELEBRATING

REPAIRING THE BREACH ★ RAISING THE STANDARD

★ REAPING THE HARVEST ★

20th ANNIVERSARY

COVENANT
BLESSINGS
Of
God's Nature

COVENANT BLESSINGS OF
GOD'S NATURE

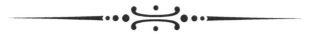

HIS DEFENSE AGAINST OUR ENEMIES

He delivereth me from mine enemies: yea, thou liftest me up above those that rise up against me: thou hast delivered me from the violent man (Psalm 18:48).

Though I walk in the midst of trouble, thou wilt revive me: thou shalt stretch forth thine hand against the wrath of mine enemies, and thy right hand shall save me (Psalm 138:7).

Blessed be the Lord my strength, which teacheth my hands to war, and my fingers to fight: My goodness, and my fortress; my high tower, and my deliverer; my shield, and he in whom I trust; who subdueth my people under me (Psalm 144:1,2).

I will deliver thee out of the hand of the wicked, and I will redeem thee out of the hand of the terrible (Jeremiah 15:21).

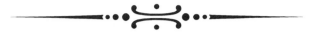

When you know the strategies of Satan he cannot take you by surprise. When you understand there is a spiritual war going on, you will not be vulnerable to the attack of the enemy.

Greater is my God who is in me, in front of me, behind me, beside me, beneath me and above me than the devil that is in the world.

We are invading enemy-held territory with all the arsenal of God at our disposal; yet while some are brandishing swords and spears, others are waving butter knives.

The defense of God against our adversary can be seen in the activity of the eagle. With eyelids that shade the ultraviolet rays of the sun, the eagle flies sunward when pursued, blinding his enemy.

When the adversary pursues you, don't run toward the darkness, but, rather, toward the radiant light of the Son of God. As you run you can see God, but your adversary just sees the light, is overwhelmed and is unable to find you.

COVENANT BLESSINGS OF GOD'S NATURE

HIS GRACE

For as by one man's disobedience many were made sinners, so by the obedience of one shall many be made righteous. Moreover the law entered, that the offence might abound. But where sin abounded, grace did much more abound: That as sin hath reigned unto death, even so might grace reign through righteousness unto eternal life by Jesus Christ our Lord (Romans 5:19-21).

For sin shall not have dominion over you: for ye are not under the law, but under grace (Romans 6:14).

And God is able to make all grace abound toward you; that ye, always having all sufficiency in all things, may abound to every good work (2 Corinthians 9:8).

For by grace are ye saved through faith; and that not of yourselves: it is the gift of God (Ephesians 2:8).

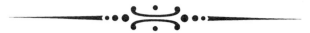

Grace is the availability of God's power to deliver you. Have you ever looked at yourself in the mirror in the middle of your greatest tragedy? There you felt the onslaught of the alien armies of the Antichrist and said, "I don't know how I can lift my hands and praise Him! Everything around me is falling apart, but I am not!" Why? Because grace is upon you to get you through whatever it is God is calling you to walk through!

The grace of God is endless, and the battle scars we acquire throughout our walk are nothing more than reminders of His amazing grace.

We are all sinners, deserving to spend eternity amidst the howls and the cackles of a devil's hell! This is the destiny we justly deserve and that truth demands. But just before truth's gavel strikes, and the sentence is pronounced guilty, see it apprehended in mid-air by the hand of grace. See Him stay the hand of judgment and move Himself between judgment and you.

The more basic the truth the more profound the impact. How marvelous grace must be that God should love a sinner such as me!

COVENANT BLESSINGS OF GOD'S NATURE

HIS LOVE

The Lord hath appeared of old unto me, saying, Yea, I have loved thee with an everlasting love: therefore with lovingkindness have I drawn thee (Jeremiah 31:3).

Who shall separate us from the love of Christ? shall tribulation, or distress, or persecution, or famine, or nakedness, or peril, or sword? As it is written, For thy sake we are killed all the day long; we are accounted as sheep for the slaughter. Nay, in all these things we are more than conquerors through him that loved us. For I am persuaded, that neither death, nor life, nor angels, nor principalities, nor powers, nor things present, nor things to come, Nor height, nor depth, nor any other creature, shall be able to separate us from the love of God, which is in Christ Jesus our Lord (Romans 8:35-39).

Herein is love, not that we loved God, but that he loved us, and sent his Son to be the propitiation for our sins (1 John 4:10).

INSPIRING INSIGHTS
by Rod Parsley

If you put all of God's characteristics into a pot and boiled them down, they would boil down to one all-encompassing element of His divine nature: LOVE.

The Bible declares that the foundation and bedrock of our lives is built upon three things: faith, hope and love. These three shall remain.

If you have faith and hope without love, you don't have a lasting relationship. If you have love and hope without faith, then you have criticism, skepticism and fear. If you have faith and love without hope, then you have despair! When trouble comes without hope as your foundation, you will give up and quit. But the greatest of these is love.

I would rather be a beggar in the streets and have Jesus in my soul, than to own the riches and wealth of this world and be separated from the love of God.

Jesus loved us so much that He refused to live without us. He died so He could make us His own!

11

COVENANT BLESSINGS OF
GOD'S NATURE

HIS MERCY

Good and upright is the Lord: therefore will he teach sinners in the way. All the paths of the Lord are mercy and truth unto such as keep his covenant and his testimonies (Psalm 25:8,10).

It is of the Lord's mercies that we are not consumed, because his compassions fail not. They are new every morning: great is thy faithfulness (Lamentations 3:22,23).

Blessed are the merciful: for they shall obtain mercy (Matthew 5:7).

But ye are a chosen generation, a royal priesthood, an holy nation, a peculiar people; that ye should shew forth the praises of him who hath called you out of darkness into his marvellous light: Which in time past were not a people, but are now the people of God: which had not obtained mercy, but now have obtained mercy (1 Peter 2:9,10).

Mercy climbed onto a chariot, rode high upon the forever mountain and picked up the Son of God. He came rolling across the Milky Way amid the stars and planets. He came swirling by the graveyard of humanity and became the propitiation for our sins forever, to abolish Justice and the Law.

The crowd wrenched the beard from Jesus' face. Mercy's blood ran freely down His naked side and dripped into bloody pools on the earth. Mercy said, "Father, forgive them; for they know not what they do" (Luke 23:34). Death rode back and forth on a pale horse at the base of Calvary, until finally he stormed up Golgotha's hillside.

The virgin's Son died. They took His lifeless body from off the Cross, His flesh hanging like ribbons, His brow beaten. They wrapped Him in grave clothes, and laid Him in a borrowed tomb.

But on the third day Mercy came out of the tomb. And there was a great earthquake, for an angel descended from heaven, rolled back the stone and sat upon it. His countenance was like lightning, and His raiment was white as snow. The declaration was made, "Jesus is not here, He is risen as He said." That is Mercy's message.

COVENANT BLESSINGS OF GOD'S NATURE

HIS PEACE

Great peace have they which love thy law: and nothing shall offend them (Psalm 119:165).

When a man's ways please the Lord, he maketh even his enemies to be at peace with him (Proverb 16:7).

Thou wilt keep him in perfect peace, whose mind is stayed on thee: because he trusteth in thee (Isaiah 26:3).

Peace I leave with you, my peace I give unto you: not as the world giveth, give I unto you. Let not your heart be troubled, neither let it be afraid (John 14:27).

And the peace of God, which passeth all understanding, shall keep your hearts and minds through Christ Jesus (Philippians 4:7).

When you are at peace you are settled in your mind, vision and purpose. Peace is internal, not external. Freedom from conflict is not your peace. Jesus is your peace.

The kingdom of God consists of peace. It is peace that transcends human understanding. It is a peace that cannot be bought; the peace that cannot come with fame; the peace that cannot come with anything that this world affords.

Jehovah Shalom, the God of Peace, will supernaturally give you peace. He desires to make peace a banner that will fly over you as a memorial. When striving begins, peace will come.

When your life is spinning out of control and everything you are doing just seems to drive you further away from God's presence, it is then that the Prince of Peace bursts forth onto the scene.

At that moment all your striving will cease, and everything you have worked so hard to accomplish will suddenly come to pass. The peace of God will flood your life, as you look around at all the disarray, and you will not even be moved!

COVENANT BLESSINGS OF GOD'S NATURE

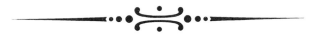

HIS WILL

For I know the thoughts that I think toward you, saith the Lord, thoughts of peace, and not of evil, to give you an expected end (Jeremiah 29:11).

For this cause we also, since the day we heard it, do not cease to pray for you, and to desire that ye might be filled with the knowledge of his will in all wisdom and spiritual understanding (Colossians 1:9).

Cast not away therefore your confidence, which hath great recompence of reward. For ye have need of patience, that, after ye have done the will of God, ye might receive the promise (Hebrews 10:35,36).

And this is the confidence that we have in him, that, if we ask any thing according to his will, he heareth us: And if we know that he heareth us: whatsoever we ask, we know that we have the petitions that we desired of him (1 John 5:14,15).

INSPIRING INSIGHTS
by Rod Parsley

You can no longer question the will of God for your situation. You have His word concerning His will. It is salvation—healing, deliverance and well being in every area of your life.

If you ask anything, according to His will, He hears you. In other words, God, in eternity past, already set His will in motion, made the divine decision and sealed it by the Holy Ghost and by the blood of the Lamb. He, in essence, said, "Whatever you pray, I already will to hear you, and because I hear you, I shall answer you."

So many times we, as Christians, go around saying, "Lord, what is your will?" Understanding and knowing the will of God for your life is very simple. It is birthed out of prayer and a daily relationship with the Lord.

The will of God is not something you find, it is something you live. Right now you are in the circumference of the will of God for your life. Through a series of seemingly insignificant events, God will lead you from where you are to where you need to be.

COVENANT BLESSINGS OF GOD'S NATURE

OUR ADVOCATE

Who shall lay any thing to the charge of God's elect? It is God that justifieth. Who is he that condemneth? It is Christ that died, yea rather, that is risen again, who is even at the right hand of God, who also maketh intercession for us (Romans 8:33,34).

But this man [Jesus], because he continueth ever, hath an unchangeable priesthood. Wherefore he is able also to save them to the uttermost that come unto God by him, seeing he ever liveth to make intercession for them (Hebrews 7:24,25).

My little children, these things write I unto you, that ye sin not. And if any man sin, we have an advocate with the Father, Jesus Christ the righteous: And he is the propitiation for our sins: and not for ours only, but also for the sins of the whole world (1 John 2:1,2).

INSPIRING INSIGHTS
by Rod Parsley

We have a Great Advocate—in Jesus Christ. And supernaturally He is praying for you and me 24 hours a day, because He is not bound or limited by the physical realm!

Our advocate—the same Holy Spirit that invaded the borrowed tomb of Joseph of Arimathea and raised the three-day dead body of Jesus of Nazareth from the dead—is inside you right now praying for you and your every need!

Jesus Christ is your Advocate or your attorney. He is not one who will get you off when you are right. That isn't much of an attorney.

Rather, you have an attorney, in the person of the Resurrected Savior, who will plead your case when you are wrong. He will stand before our Father in heaven and point at His crimson blood, which covers the Mercy Seat. In spite of your guilt, the great Judge of the universe will hand down a "not guilty" verdict, even when He knows you are guilty. You have an Advocate!

You may be guilty, but—because of Jesus' blood—you are also blameless! He doesn't hold anything against you! In the corridors of heaven, no diabolic accusation by the demonic forces of the devil's domain are a match for your Advocate!

COVENANT BLESSINGS OF GOD'S NATURE

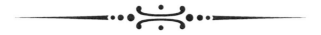

OUR ANSWER

Give ear, O Lord, unto my prayer; and attend to the voice of my supplications. In the day of my trouble I will call upon thee: for thou wilt answer me (Psalm 86:6,7).

And it shall come to pass, that before they call, I will answer; and while they are yet speaking, I will hear (Isaiah 65:23,24).

Call unto me, and I will answer thee, and shew thee great and mighty things, which thou knowest not (Jeremiah 33:3).

Have faith in God. For verily I say unto you, That whosoever shall say unto this mountain, be thou removed, and be thou cast into the sea; and shall not doubt in his heart, but shall believe that those things which he saith shall come to pass; he shall have whatsoever he saith. Therefore I say unto you, What things soever ye desire, when ye pray, believe that ye receive them, and ye shall have them (Mark 11:22-24).

God never refuses to answer scriptural prayers! In fact, He has already said in His Word, "It is my will to hear you!" God is listening for you! So you say it and then you shall have it!

What do you do in the interim? You cast not away your fearless confidence, for it has great recompense of reward. You have need, your Bible says, of patience after that you have done the will of God, that you might inherit the promise (Hebrews 10:36)! You have to do something while you are standing! Fight the fight of faith!

I don't know where we came up with this God that doesn't answer prayer. I have searched the Bible from cover to cover, and all I can find is a God that says, "You have not because you ask not" (James 4:2).

You serve a prayer answering God. You have yet to pray the prayer that He did not answer the very moment your petition was heard around the throne. Immediately, He dispatched a legion of angels to meet your need. God's divine edict still declares, "What things soever ye desire, when ye pray, believe ye receive them, and ye shall have them" (Mark 11:24).

COVENANT BLESSINGS OF GOD'S NATURE

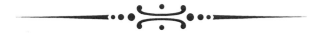

OUR FRIEND

A man that hath friends must shew himself friendly: and there is a friend that sticketh closer than a brother (Proverb 18:24).

The Son of man came eating and drinking, and they say, Behold a man gluttonous, and a winebibber, a friend of publicans and sinners. But wisdom is justified of her children (Matthew 11:19).

Ye are my friends, if ye do whatsoever I command you. Henceforth I call you not servants; for the servant knoweth not what his Lord doeth: but I have called you friends; for all things that I have heard of my Father I have made known unto you (John 15:14,15).

And the scripture was fulfilled which saith, Abraham believed God, and it was imputed unto him for righteousness: and he was called the Friend of God (James 2:23).

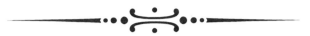

Jesus is a friend who sticks closer than any friend or family member. Even in your darkest hour of sin He is known as the friend of sinners!

Those words, spoken as an insult by the religious crowd of Jesus' day, have become the testimony of every hurting person. What was meant as a criticism has become the cradle of blessing for a sin-sick world.

Our Risen Savior did not send a prescription, stand back, point His finger and command you to do better. He wouldn't do that to a friend. Instead, He rolled up His sleeves, called eternity, wrapped Himself in flesh and bone, left the pavilions of glory and dwelt among us . . . the only Begotten of the Father (John 1:14).

Jesus could have laid down His friendship with us and picked up the robe of royalty. But I believe He said to His Father, "I've walked where they have walked, and I know the burdens of their hearts." He is interceding for you and me and your lost loved ones right now. He is petitioning the throne of God for the very thing that keeps you up at night. Jesus has not forgotten you!

COVENANT BLESSINGS OF
GOD'S NATURE

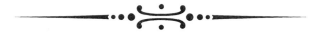

OUR HELP

Our soul waiteth for the Lord: he is our help and our shield. For our heart shall rejoice in him, because we have trusted in his holy name (Psalm 33:20,21)

God is our refuge and strength, a very present help in trouble. Therefore will not we fear, though the earth be removed, and though the mountains be carried into the midst of the sea; though the waters thereof roar and be troubled, though the mountains shake with the swelling thereof. Selah (Psalm 46:1-3).

I will lift up mine eyes unto the hills, from whence cometh my help. My help cometh from the Lord, which made heaven and earth. He will not suffer thy foot to be moved: he that keepeth thee will not slumber (Psalm 121:1-3).

Let us therefore come boldly unto the throne of grace, that we may obtain mercy, and find grace to help in time of need (Hebrews 4:16).

INSPIRING INSIGHTS
by Rod Parsley

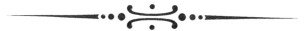

It is impossible to be led without our Helper, the Lord Jesus Christ. You can't be what God wants you to be without His help, and He wants nothing more than to see you succeed!

The Lord is your helper! He is your help in the hour of temptation. He is your rescue squad with limitless capabilities to save you. He is the help for your family. The help that you need is living in you right now!

So many times we are busy looking to everyone and everything else, except Jesus, to deliver us in our most desperate hour of need. But we have already been provided with an arsenal in the person of our risen Savior, Jesus Christ, the helper of our souls.

As we stay focused on Him, He will meet our every need and provide us with help and hope.

The Lord is ever present and willing to help in your most desperate hour of need!

COVENANT BLESSINGS OF
GOD'S NATURE

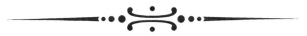

THE LORD OUR HEALER

If thou wilt diligently hearken to the voice of the Lord thy God, and wilt do that which is right in his sight, and wilt give ear to his commandments, and keep all his statutes, I will put none of these diseases upon thee, which I have brought upon the Egyptians: for I am the Lord that healeth thee (Exodus 15:26).

Bless the Lord, O my soul, and forget not all his benefits: who forgiveth all thine iniquities; who healeth all thy diseases; who redeemeth thy life from destruction; who crowneth thee with lovingkindness and tender mercies; who satisfieth thy mouth with good things; so that thy youth is renewed like the eagle's (Psalm 103:2-5).

The Spirit of the Lord is upon me, because he hath anointed me to preach the gospel to the poor; he hath sent me to heal the brokenhearted, to preach deliverance to the captives, and recovering of sight to the blind, to set at liberty them that are bruised, to preach the acceptable year of the Lord (Luke 4:18,19).

Jesus is not only the Physician of your body, but also He is the Physician of your mind and your spirit. He provided the cure, through the Cross of Calvary, to cleanse you of whatever ails you. He wants to take control of your situation. He wants to touch you where others have failed to do so.

Calvary's double cure is salvation and healing through the spotless blood of Jesus Christ, the only begotten Son of God.

Through the filter of a blood covering, God, our Great Physician, treated the symptoms for both sin and sickness.

On the backside of Calvary, between Christ and the Cross, the miraculous began. Jesus' wound flowed against the skin of the tree. A crimson stain marked the post, thereby initiating God's redeeming passover of man's sickness.

You don't need a healing, you need the Healer. Jesus is the answer to every prayer you will ever pray.

COVENANT BLESSINGS OF GOD'S NATURE

THE LORD OUR SHEPHERD

The Lord is my shepherd; I shall not want. He maketh me to lie down in green pastures: he leadeth me beside the still waters. He restoreth my soul: he leadeth me in the paths of righteousness for his name's sake. Yea, though I walk through the valley of the shadow of death, I will fear no evil: for thou art with me; thy rod and thy staff they comfort me. Thou preparest a table before me in the presence of mine enemies: thou anointest my head with oil; my cup runneth over. Surely goodness and mercy shall follow me all the days of my life: and I will dwell in the house of the Lord for ever (Psalm 23:1-6).

I am the good shepherd, and know my sheep, and am known of mine (John 10:14).

Now the God of peace . . . that great shepherd of the sheep . . . Make you perfect in every good work to do his will, working in you that which is well-pleasing in his sight, through Jesus Christ; to whom be glory for ever and ever. Amen (Hebrews 13:20,21).

One of the names of God is Jehovah Rohi, the Lord God is our shepherd. When you really know Him as your Shepherd, you won't have to do half as much warring, because the Shepherd will lead you and guide you!

Psalm 23 says, "The Lord is my Shepherd . . . Thy rod and thy staff they comfort me." Tomorrow will be no surprise to God. Do not fear tomorrow, for the Lord of Glory has gone before you into the future and prepared a way for you where there was no way. He has brought your mountains low, and your valleys He has exalted.

As a shepherd goes before his sheep, Jesus will lead you through narrow passageways where your adversary waits. Therefore, with a rod and staff, He will drive away your enemies and open a way for you to follow Him.

Our God broke the power of death and said, "Come and follow me." He's the first begotten of the dead. We do not fear death or destruction, because our God has conquered them.

ROD PARSLEY CELEBRATING
REPAIRING THE BREACH • RAISING THE STANDARD
• REAPING THE HARVEST •

20th ANNIVERSARY

COVENANT BLESSINGS Through Jesus Christ

COVENANT BLESSINGS THROUGH JESUS CHRIST

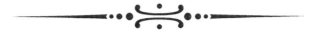

POWER OF ADOPTION

But as many as received him [Jesus], to them gave he power to become the sons of God, even to them that believe on his name: Which were born, not of blood, nor of the will of the flesh, nor of the will of man, but of God (John 1:12,13).

For as many as are led by the Spirit of God, they are the sons of God. For ye have not received the spirit of bondage again to fear; but ye have received the Spirit of adoption, whereby we cry, Abba, Father. The Spirit itself beareth witness with our spirit, that we are the children of God (Romans 8:14-16).

But when the fulness of the time was come, God sent forth his Son, made of a woman, made under the law, to redeem them that were under the law, that we might receive the adoption of sons. And because ye are sons, God hath sent forth the Spirit of his Son into your hearts, crying, Abba, Father. Wherefore thou art no more a servant, but a son; and if a son, then an heir of God through Christ (Galatians 4:4-7).

INSPIRING INSIGHTS
by Rod Parsley

The act of treason by Adam and Eve in bygone millennia wound man's moral clock backwards. Sin caused a great chasm between humanity and our loving heavenly Father. Since then, God has been devising a plan to return us to our original state of affairs and adopt us back into His royal family.

❖❖❖

When you were redeemed, you received salvation, regeneration and right standing with God. But in adoption you don't just find a new place, you find a new position. You then have a legal standing, because you have been adopted.

When you are adopted, you are released from the obligations of your previous family. Whoever they owed, you don't owe any longer. Whatever they did is not a part of you any longer.

You don't have to bow your knee to poverty, shame, sickness, malady or malfunction. You have been released from the obligations of the human family and adopted into the family of God!

❖❖❖

When adopted by God, you gain the rights and privileges of the family to which you have been adopted. You receive the name of Jesus and all the power and authority that goes with it!

COVENANT BLESSINGS THROUGH JESUS CHRIST

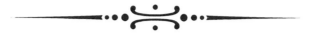

POWER OF HIS BLOOD

For all have sinned, and come short of the glory of God; being justified freely by his grace through the redemption that is in Christ Jesus: Whom God hath set forth to be a propitiation through faith in his blood, to declare his righteousness for the remission of sins that are past, through the forbearance of God (Romans 3:23-25).

But Christ being come an high priest of good things to come, by a greater and more perfect tabernacle, not made with hands, that is to say, not of this building; For if the blood of bulls and of goats, and the ashes of an heifer sprinkling the unclean, sanctifieth to the purifying of the flesh: how much more shall the blood of Christ, who through the eternal Spirit offered himself without spot to God, purge your conscience from dead works to serve the living God (Hebrews 9:11-14)?

And they overcame him by the blood of the Lamb, and by the word of their testimony; and they loved not their lives unto the death (Revelation 12:11).

There is no salvation in a Shinto shrine or a Buddhist temple. I am not ashamed to tell you that there is only one way to God, and that is through the blood of His only Son.

Sin-infected humanity needed the kind of blood transfusion only God could provide. The only way such a divine exchange could be made was for God Himself to provide the blood.

You are redeemed by the blood of the Lamb. It is not by your works. It is not by your deeds. It is not by your good name. It is not by your standing in the community. It is not by your checking account or your credit rating. It is not who you know and do not know. It is only by the blood—the great equalizer.

The blood of Jesus is for more than just to save your soul from hell. It is for protection, salvation, healing, deliverance and provision. When you plead the blood of the Lamb, do it with authority and confidence. The forces of darkness cannot cross the line of the shed blood of Jesus, slain from the foundation of the world!

COVENANT BLESSINGS THROUGH JESUS CHRIST

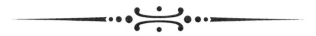

POWER OF HIS COVENANT

And I will make an everlasting covenant with them. And their seed shall be known among the Gentiles, and their offspring among the people: all that see them shall acknowledge them, that they are the seed which the Lord hath blessed (Isaiah 61:8,9).

For if that first covenant had been faultless, then should no place have been sought for the second. For finding fault with them, he saith, Behold, the days come, saith the Lord, when I will make a new covenant with the house of Israel and with the house of Judah: not according to the covenant that I made with their fathers in the day when I took them by the hand to lead them out of the land of Egypt; because they continued not in my covenant, and I regarded them not, saith the Lord. For this is the covenant that I will make with the house of Israel after those days, saith the Lord; I will put my laws into their mind, and write them in their hearts: and I will be to them a God, and they shall be to me a people (Hebrews 8:7-10).

INSPIRING INSIGHTS
by Rod Parsley

God looked for a covenant that could not be annulled. He looked for a covenant that all the demons in the darkened regions of the devil's abyss could never break. God looked for a covenant that sin as black as midnight was unable to drown out. God sent His Son, spotless and holy. Jesus shed blood that had never been tainted with the stench of sin. God and His Son together cut a covenant.

In that covenant He said, this promise is not for me only, but for you and for your children after you . . . and to as many as the Lord our God shall call. What is He saying? This is a blood covenant that can never be broken.

When you fail, God doesn't frown. He just says, "Look upon what used to be known as the judgment seat. Look at the sprinkling of the blood. There is the covenant." The covenant is not between you and God. The covenant is between God and His Son. It cannot fail, and, by coming into this covenant through salvation, neither can you!

COVENANT BLESSINGS THROUGH JESUS CHRIST

POWER OF HIS CROSS

For the preaching of the cross is to them that perish foolishness; but unto us which are saved it is the power of God (1 Corinthians 1:18).

And you, being dead in your sins and the uncircumcision of your flesh, hath he quickened together with him, having forgiven you all trespasses; blotting out the handwriting of ordinances that was against us, which was contrary to us, and took it out of the way, nailing it to his cross; and having spoiled principalities and powers, he made a shew of them openly, triumphing over them in it (Colossians 2:13-15).

But God forbid that I should glory, save in the cross of our Lord Jesus Christ, by whom the world is crucified unto me, and I unto the world. And as many as walk according to this rule, peace be on them, and mercy, and upon the Israel of God (Galatians 6:14,16).

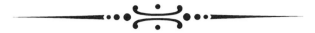

There is enough power in the cross of Jesus Christ to keep you from falling. There is enough power in Jesus' blood, shed on that cross, to keep you so that every time sin knocks on the door of your heart, faith answers.

The Cross gives you victory over sin. It is not provided by your righteousness. Your righteousness is as filthy rags. You are crucified with Him, nevertheless you live, yet not you, but Christ liveth in you (Galatians 2:20).

Jesus went from the cradle to the cross in order to give you victory and hope. You only have one adversary. There is only one entity standing between you and absolute victory in every area of your life—Satan. But on the cross Jesus put one foot on the devil's head and defeated all the forces of darkness so that you could have life.

Salvation is by grace and comes by the blood of the cross of Christ, nothing more and nothing less.

COVENANT BLESSINGS THROUGH JESUS CHRIST

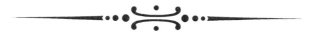

POWER OF HIS FORGIVENESS

If thou, Lord, shouldest mark iniquities, O Lord, who shall stand? But there is forgiveness with thee, that thou mayest be feared (Psalm 130:3,4).

And when ye stand praying, forgive, if ye have ought against any: that your Father also which is in heaven may forgive you your trespasses (Mark 11:25).

Blessed is the man to whom the Lord will not impute sin (Romans 4:8).

But if we walk in the light, as he is in the light, we have fellowship one with another, and the blood of Jesus Christ his Son cleanseth us from all sin. If we say that we have no sin, we deceive ourselves, and the truth is not in us. If we confess our sins, he is faithful and just to forgive us our sins, and to cleanse us from all unrighteousness (1 John 1:7-9).

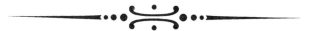

Forgiveness buries sin deeper than deception.

At what time did God ever tag a "yeah, but" on the end of His forgiveness toward you? How much did you have to go through in order for you to receive absolute forgiveness? God's forgiveness never fails or runs out for you.

There is forgiveness through Jesus Christ. His grace has never been exhausted. His forgiveness has never even been diluted of its original strength. When one precious drop of the Prince of God's blood spilled over Calvary's hillside, all humanity's sins, forever past and forever future, were swallowed in the flood tide of the forgiving blood of the crucified Lamb of God!

The major purpose of Jesus is forgiveness. You are a vessel through whom a way for sinful man has been provided to receive His forgiveness.

When you confess your sins, you are forgiven at that moment. Your sins are forgiven and forgotten, never to be remembered again.

COVENANT BLESSINGS THROUGH JESUS CHRIST

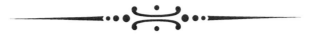

POWER OF RECONCILIATION

For if, when we were enemies, we were reconciled to God by the death of his Son, much more, being reconciled, we shall be saved by his life. And not only so, but we also joy in God through our Lord Jesus Christ, by whom we have now received the atonement (Romans 5:10,11).

If any man be in Christ, he is a new creature: old things are passed away; behold, all things are become new. And all things are of God, who hath reconciled us to himself by Jesus Christ, and hath given to us the ministry of reconciliation (2 Corinthians 5:17,18).

For it pleased the Father that in him should all fulness dwell; and, having made peace through the blood of his cross, by him to reconcile all things unto himself; by him, I say, whether they be things in earth, or things in heaven. And you, that were sometime alienated and enemies in your mind by wicked works, yet now hath he reconciled (Colossians 1:19-21).

INSPIRING INSIGHTS
by Rod Parsley

God sees every person in this world. He has already provided for your freedom. Nowhere can you find God, after the cross and the resurrection, trying to get reconciled to man. Through those acts He provided a way for all men to be gloriously saved and in right relationship with Him.

God has already reconciled Himself to us through Jesus Christ. He is just waiting for humanity to go through the open door and accept this reconciliation.

Reconciliation translated means mutually changed. God's love, which had been pent up behind the wall of man's sin, was released at Calvary toward us, and judgment was satisfied. The human race can now be free.

The Holy God gives us free access into His presence! The veil that hung in the temple, four-inches thick, woven without a seam, twenty-feet wide, and forty-feet high, was torn from top to bottom by God, and He said, "I am coming out, and you are coming in."

COVENANT BLESSINGS THROUGH JESUS CHRIST

POWER OF HIS WORD

For as the rain cometh down, and the snow from heaven, and returneth not thither, but watereth the earth, and maketh it bring forth and bud, that it may give seed to the sower, and bread to the eater: so shall my word be that goeth forth out of my mouth: it shall not return unto me void, but it shall accomplish that which I please, and it shall prosper in the thing whereto I sent it (Isaiah 55:10,11).

That if thou shalt confess with thy mouth the Lord Jesus, and shalt believe in thine heart that God hath raised him from the dead, thou shalt be saved (Romans 10:9).

For the word of God is quick, and powerful, and sharper than any two-edged sword, piercing even to the dividing asunder of soul and spirit, and of the joints and marrow, and is a discerner of the thoughts and intents of the heart (Hebrews 4:12).

INSPIRING INSIGHTS
by Rod Parsley

If the Lord and His Word never change, and if He created life with a spoken word, then He is still able to speak into existence whatever you need today.

When the world is dying and the moon is bleeding, and the seas are seething under the whiplash of the fury of God, there is still a rock of safety and a place of refuge! It is called the Word of God, and you have it right now.

Your most effective weapon in answering God's call to victory is the Bible. The strategy and training for battle is found in His Word. In fact, the rifle for your battle is God's Word.

I envision an army of God so equipped with His Word that they live with it, eat with it, sleep with it and use it every moment of every day. We have the weapon; it is time to use it constantly. With three simple words from the Bible, Jesus defeated the devil in the wilderness. He said simply, "It is written." We have that power also.

COVENANT
BLESSINGS
for
Equipping the Saints

COVENANT BLESSINGS FOR EQUIPPING THE SAINTS

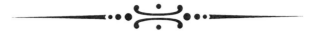

ANOINTING

Thou lovest righteousness, and hatest wickedness: therefore God, thy God, hath anointed thee with the oil of gladness above thy fellows (Psalm 45:7).

For, lo, thine enemies, O Lord, for, lo, thine enemies shall perish; all the workers of iniquity shall be scattered. But my horn shalt thou exalt like the horn of an unicorn: I shall be anointed with fresh oil (Psalm 92:9,10).

And it shall come to pass in that day, that his burden shall be taken away from off thy shoulder, and his yoke from off thy neck, and the yoke shall be destroyed because of the anointing (Isaiah 10:27).

But the anointing which ye have received of him abideth in you, and ye need not that any man teach you: but as the same anointing teacheth you of all things, and is truth, and is no lie, and even as it hath taught you, ye shall abide in him (1 John 2:27).

INSPIRING INSIGHTS
by Rod Parsley

The world doesn't need another gifted man. It is looking for an anointed, yielded man.

The anointing is the tangible presence of God to destroy the yoke of bondage in your life. It is the touch of the Holy Spirit to loose you from every bondage. It is the transference of His power to remove every burden. It is the anointing to set you free in every area of your life!

The anointing is like a spiritual deodorant. It is a safeguard against the attack of rotten, stinking sin.

❖❖❖

The anointing of God lives on the inside of you, because the Anointed One lives on the inside of you. And, with Him you receive supernatural ability. You are not anointed to feel good; you are anointed to meet the needs of lost and hurting humanity.

You have an unction or an anointing. It is a perpetual propulsion of the power of God to break you through every line of Satan's defense.

COVENANT BLESSINGS FOR EQUIPPING THE SAINTS

BAPTISM OF THE HOLY SPIRIT

And it shall come to pass afterward, that I will pour out my spirit upon all flesh; and your sons and your daughters shall prophesy, your old men shall dream dreams, your young men shall see visions: And also upon the servants and upon the handmaids in those days will I pour out my spirit (Joel 2:28,29).

But the Comforter, which is the Holy Ghost, whom the Father will send in my name, he shall teach you all things, and bring all things to your remembrance, whatsoever I have said unto you (John 14:26).

And when the day of Pentecost was fully come, they were all with one accord in one place. And suddenly there came a sound from heaven as of a rushing mighty wind, and it filled all the house where they were sitting. And there appeared unto them cloven tongues like as of fire, and it sat upon each of them. And they were all filled with the Holy Ghost, and began to speak with other tongues, as the Spirit gave them utterance (Acts 2:1-4).

Someone somewhere will duplicate the book of Acts, and when they do, the book of Acts will pale in comparison and look like a Sunday school picnic. I want to be that person.

In Matthew, Mark, Luke and John we see the God in Christ . . . but in the book of Acts the God in Christ becomes the Christ in you!

Perhaps the first voice to ever utter "power to the people" was the Holy Spirit as He rode into the city on the very breath of God.

The baptism in the Holy Ghost will do for you what a phone booth did for Clark Kent—it will change you into another human being.

In a time when a powerless Pentecost has been the norm and not the exception, with more perversion than power, more playboys than prophets and more compromise than conviction—we need the Holy Ghost, who condescends to indwell mortals and fill us full of Himself.

COVENANT BLESSINGS FOR EQUIPPING THE SAINTS

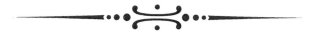

PRAISE TO GOD

And they rose early in the morning, and went forth into the wilderness of Tekoa: and as they went forth, Jehoshaphat stood and said, Hear me, O Judah, and ye inhabitants of Jerusalem; Believe in the Lord your God, so shall ye be established; believe his prophets, so shall ye prosper.

And when he had consulted with the people, he appointed singers unto the Lord, and that should praise the beauty of holiness, as they went out before the army, and to say, Praise the Lord; for his mercy endureth for ever.

And when they began to sing and to praise, the Lord set ambushments against the children of Ammon, Moab, and mount Seir, which were come against Judah; and they were smitten (2 Chronicles 20:20-22).

I will bless the Lord at all times: his praise shall continually be in my mouth. My soul shall make her boast in the Lord: the humble shall hear thereof, and be glad. O magnify the Lord with me, and let us exalt his name together. I sought the Lord, and he heard me, and delivered me from all my fears (Psalm 34:1-4).

INSPIRING INSIGHTS
by Rod Parsley

Praise is to speak forth and declare the Word of the Lord in every situation. Whatever you are praising and believing God for, according to His will, you shall have it. And, the *I shall* becomes the *I will* as the manifestation of your miracle comes forth in your life.

❖❖❖

As you praise God, you are literally placing a weapon of war in His hand to destroy your adversary and bring ultimate victory!

Like Paul and Silas in the Roman prison, those who sing in prison can never truly be bound. Those who sing praises continually will never cease to fulfill their destiny. Praise changes things. It is the hinge upon which the door of worship swings open.

Praise stills the avenger. Every time you lift up a "Hallelujah," shout "Amen" or sing "Amazing Grace," praise, like a sweet smelling savor, goes before the throne of God . . . and He comes to consume that praise and carry you into the glory of His presence so that you may partake of His richest blessings.

COVENANT BLESSINGS FOR EQUIPPING THE SAINTS

PRAYER TO GOD

If my people, which are called by my name, shall humble themselves, and pray, and seek my face, and turn from their wicked ways; then will I hear from heaven, and will forgive their sin, and will heal their land (2 Chronicles 7:14).

And he [Jesus] spake a parable unto them to this end, that men ought always to pray, and not to faint (Luke 18:1).

Likewise the Spirit also helpeth our infirmities: for we know not what we should pray for as we ought: but the Spirit itself maketh intercession for us with groanings which cannot be uttered (Romans 8:26).

Confess your faults one to another, and pray one for another, that ye may be healed. The effectual fervent prayer of a righteous man availeth much (James 5:16).

INSPIRING INSIGHTS
by Rod Parsley

Throughout our lives we have been taught prayer consists of kneeling down, folding our hands and going through the rudiments of religion. All of these acts have their place and purpose in prayer, but they are not true prayer.

Prayer, in its simplest form, means to aspire toward the supreme end. Summed up, it is not my will but the declaration that God's will be done. In other words, I consciously will that the ultimate purpose of God's kingdom—the full purpose of God in every endeavor, thought and motive—be established in my life.

Christians who always pray do not faint, and Christians who faint do so at the neglect of prayer.

❖❖❖

You have never prayed the prayer that God did not hear and answer immediately. When Daniel bowed his head and prayed for twenty-one days and received no answer, he said, "Lord, haven't you heard your servant's cry?"

God responded, "An angel was sent from my presence that same day, but the Prince of Darkness withstood him; then the angel overthrew him." And I can hear Daniel say, "There's power in prayer."

COVENANT BLESSINGS FOR EQUIPPING THE SAINTS

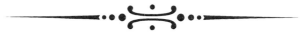

SERVICE TO GOD AND THE BODY OF CHRIST

Mine eyes shall be upon the faithful of the land, that they may dwell with me: he that walketh in a perfect way, he shall serve me (Psalm 101:6).

If any man serve me, let him follow me; and where I am, there shall also my servant be: if any man serve me, him will my Father honour (John 12:26).

And whatsoever ye do, do it heartily, as to the Lord, and not unto men; Knowing that of the Lord ye shall receive the reward of the inheritance: for ye serve the Lord Christ (Colossians 3:23,24).

For God is not unrighteous to forget your work and labour of love, which ye have shewed toward his name, in that ye have ministered to the saints, and do minister (Hebrews 6:10).

There is no hierarchy in the giftings of God. And ministry in the church does not rest on status, but rather it rests on service. When I serve, I have grace for the service and the servant. Every calling in the body of Christ is a calling to service.

When you come together, consider one another. This means to look at each other steadfastly with the thought in mind to serve.

What can I do for you? Can I praise Him a little better to increase the atmosphere, so you can receive your deliverance? Can I smile a little bigger to help lift your burden? Is not this the fast which God has declared unto you—the denial of self that you might loose the heavy burdens, and that the oppressed might go free? When? When you serve one another!

You may think it will cost you something to serve God, and it will. I learned at a very young age in the ministry that I could have all of God I was willing to pay for . . . it is a far greater price not to serve Him.

COVENANT BLESSINGS FOR EQUIPPING THE SAINTS

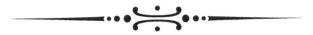

THANKSGIVING TO GOD

Offer unto God thanksgiving; and pay thy vows unto the most High: And call upon me in the day of trouble: I will deliver thee, and thou shalt glorify me (Psalm 50:14,15).

Enter into his gates with thanksgiving, and into his courts with praise: be thankful unto him, and bless his name. For the Lord is good; his mercy is everlasting; and his truth endureth to all generations (Psalm 100:4,5).

See that none render evil for evil unto any man; but ever follow that which is good, both among yourselves, and to all men. Rejoice evermore. Pray without ceasing. In every thing give thanks: for this is the will of God in Christ Jesus concerning you.

And the very God of peace sanctify you wholly; and I pray God your whole spirit and soul and body be preserved blameless unto the coming of our Lord Jesus Christ (1 Thessalonians 5:15-18,23).

Thanksgiving is when you praise God for things you can see. You thank God for your hands—you can see them. You thank God for your family—you can see them. You thank God for food. You can see it. You rejoice in the sun, the moon, the stars, the creation of God—you can see it! Thanksgiving is expressing to God your gratitude for the natural part of your daily life.

Remember when God brought the children of Israel out of Egyptian slavery? He could not take them into the Promised Land, because they were not thankful for being brought out of bondage. We must always keep a spirit of thanksgiving upon us.

Before I allow a person to complain in my presence, I often ask them to tell me ten things they are thankful for. By the time they have finished thanking God, they have forgotten why they were complaining!

❖❖❖

Thanksgiving is a sacrifice that produces the glory. If you want God to show up, be thankful. Thanksgiving is not natural, it is supernatural.

COVENANT BLESSINGS FOR EQUIPPING THE SAINTS

THE WORD OF GOD

This book of the law shall not depart out of thy mouth; but thou shalt meditate therein day and night, that thou mayest observe to do according to all that is written therein: for then thou shalt make thy way prosperous, and then thou shalt have good success (Joshua 1:8).

Blessed is the man that walketh not in the counsel of the ungodly, nor standeth in the way of sinners, nor sitteth in the seat of the scornful. But his delight is in the law of the Lord; and in his law doth he meditate day and night (Psalm 1:1,2).

Wherewithal shall a young man cleanse his way? by taking heed thereto according to thy word. Thy word have I hid in mine heart, that I might not sin against thee. Open thou mine eyes, that I may behold wondrous things out of thy law (Psalm 119:9,11,18).

Study to shew thyself approved unto God, a workman that needeth not to be ashamed, rightly dividing the word of truth (2 Timothy 2:15).

INSPIRING INSIGHTS
by Rod Parsley

To feed your spirit man, study the Word of God. Every thought and attitude must be brought into the direct spotlight of the Bible. You must read the Bible, study it and cleave to it. It is the most tangible and powerful weapon God has given us for our spiritual arsenal.

The Bible is the only source of truth. It is the only sufficient rule of faith and standard of conduct. The Bible is infallible—there are no mistakes in it—and is the inspired Word of God.

The Bible has stood for thousands of years as the number one best seller. It is still true. Trembling hands of people far greater than you and I have grasped hold of it in their dying hour. This Book will not only tell you how to live, but also it will tell you how to die! If you want to learn how to win friends and influence people, it's in there. If you need a financial plan, it's in there. Anything you need is in the Bible. It is time we returned to Bible basics.

The Word of God is like a diamond. Every time you look at it you see something different.

COVENANT BLESSINGS FOR EQUIPPING THE SAINTS

------••• ⟨⟩ •••------

WORSHIP UNTO GOD

Give unto the Lord the glory due unto his name: bring an offering, and come before him: worship the Lord in the beauty of holiness.

O give thanks unto the Lord; for he is good; for his mercy endureth for ever. And say ye, Save us, O God of our salvation, and gather us together, and deliver us from the heathen, that we may give thanks to thy holy name, and glory in thy praise. (1 Chronicles 16:29,34,35).

I will worship toward thy holy temple, and praise thy name for thy lovingkindness and for thy truth: for thou hast magnified thy word above all thy name. In the day when I cried thou answeredst me, and strengthenedst me with strength in my soul (Psalm 138:2,3).

But the hour cometh, and now is, when the true worshippers shall worship the Father in spirit and in truth: for the Father seeketh such to worship him. God is a Spirit: and they that worship him must worship him in spirit and in truth (John 4:23,24).

INSPIRING INSIGHTS
by Rod Parsley

As you enter into worship, you meet with God and He meets with you. When you get there it doesn't matter if you can't see the answer to your prayer or if there is not even the illumination of His Word to hang your faith upon—because you have Him.

It is not worship for you to sing before thousands if God's purpose for you is to work in the nursery. How many people applaud you means absolutely nothing. Purpose means everything to God.

When our hearts and motives are pure in seeking to worship God, then the world becomes a tabernacle, and living life is the incense of worship. In true worship you discover the abundant life in Christ as you yield yourself wholly to God. It is then you desire to fulfill God's purpose in every word and deed.

Let your life become the tent of meeting in which God dwells. Worship Him in spirit and truth, and allow His presence to permeate your life.

ROD PARSLEY CELEBRATING

REPAIRING THE BREACH • RAISING THE STANDARD

• REAPING THE HARVEST •

20th ANNIVERSARY

COVENANT BLESSINGS for You and Your Family

COVENANT BLESSINGS FOR
YOU AND YOUR FAMILY

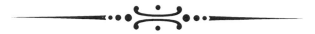

FOR THE BACKSLIDER

I have blotted out, as a thick cloud, thy transgressions, and, as a cloud, thy sins: return unto me; for I have redeemed thee (Isaiah 44:22).

Let the wicked forsake his way, and the unrighteous man his thoughts: and let him return unto the Lord, and he will have mercy upon him; and to our God, for he will abundantly pardon (Isaiah 55:7).

And I will give them an heart to know me, that I am the Lord: and they shall be my people, and I will be their God: for they shall return unto me with their whole heart (Jeremiah 24:7).

Come, and let us return unto the Lord: for he hath torn, and he will heal us; he hath smitten, and he will bind us up. Then shall we know, if we follow on to know the Lord: his going forth is prepared as the morning; and he shall come unto us as the rain, as the latter and former rain unto the earth (Hosea 6:1,3).

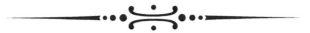

I've never seen a person who prays, reads the Bible, witnesses and goes to church backslide.

God is forever married to the backslider. What that means is He won't leave you. You have the opportunity to leave Him, but He will never leave you. And should you ever leave Him, the moment you turn around and seek Him again with your whole heart, He will be found with you.

It will cost you something to backslide. The prodigal son lost his possessions, purpose and the presence of his loving father. While covered in mud and staring at a pen full of hogs, he came to himself and headed back toward the provision and protection of home. God, like that father, stands ready to welcome every sinner home.

You can backslide before tomorrow morning if you want to. You can be drunk before midnight if you want to. God is not going to stop you, but here is the good news. While it is easy to leave the everlasting arms of God, if you don't want to, you can't be forced from His tender care. There are not enough devils to make Him give you up.

COVENANT BLESSINGS FOR YOU AND YOUR FAMILY

FOR YOUR CHILDREN

Train up a child in the way he should go: and when he is old, he will not depart from it (Proverb 22:6).

Behold, I and the children whom the Lord hath given me are for signs and for wonders in Israel from the Lord of hosts, which dwelleth in mount Zion (Isaiah 8:18).

And all thy children shall be taught of the Lord; and great shall be the peace of thy children (Isaiah 54:10,13).

And he shall turn the heart of the fathers to the children, and the heart of the children to their fathers, lest I come and smite the earth with a curse (Malachi 4:6).

Children, obey your parents in the Lord: for this is right. Honour thy father and mother; which is the first commandment with promise (Ephesians 6:1,2).

The first and highest commandment of God given to the human race is to be fruitful and multiply and replenish the earth. Why? Because the seed has that life in itself, and it reproduces after its kind.

This command is more important today than ever. Every born again, Spirit-filled believer has a responsibility to reproduce a righteous seed after their own kind. What is the righteous seed? It is our children. It is our responsibility, whether we have natural children or not, to see to it that righteous spiritual seed is reproduced in the earth. They must replenish it and subdue it for the glory of God.

The key to evangelism is not the four steps to salvation; it's the righteous seed. God is only in covenant with us as we produce the righteous seed to fulfill His purpose in the earth.

The Lord blesses those who, regardless of the cost and regardless of what it takes, will see to it that children have an opportunity to be raised up as the righteous seed of Almighty God. They will be those who change a nation and affect this final generation.

COVENANT BLESSINGS FOR YOU AND YOUR FAMILY

LOSS OF A LOVED ONE

Precious in the sight of the Lord is the death of his saints (Psalm 116:15).

So when this corruptible shall have put on incorruption, and this mortal shall have put on immortality, then shall be brought to pass the saying that is written, Death is swallowed up in victory. O death, where is thy sting? O grave, where is thy victory (1 Corinthians 15:54,55).

We are confident, I say, and willing rather to be absent from the body, and to be present with the Lord (2 Corinthians 5:8).

And I heard a great voice out of heaven saying, Behold, the tabernacle of God is with men, and he will dwell with them, and they shall be his people, and God himself shall be with them, and be their God. And God shall wipe away all tears from their eyes; and there shall be no more death, neither sorrow, nor crying, neither shall there be any more pain: for the former things are passed away (Revelation 21:3,4).

There's an old song that has encouraged me so much when the reins of death have tragically taken a friend, family member or loved one. It says, "If death should find me missing, and you don't understand, there is an old book by my bedside that will tell you where I am."

What comforting words to the saints of God. There is a hope not only in this world, but also in the world to come, and it is found in Jesus.

The temporary grief you experience when you lose a loved one is outweighed by your hope in Christ Jesus. Your loved one has joined the company of the great cloud of witnesses who are cheering you on until you also cross the threshold into the joy that has been prepared for you since the beginning of the world. (Matthew 25:34.)

In your most desperate and darkest hour of despair, darkness must give way to the dawning of a new day. The grand and glorious thought is this: you will have a great reunion with your loved one(s), and one day the tomb must give way to the resurrection power of our risen Savior!

COVENANT BLESSINGS FOR
YOU AND YOUR FAMILY

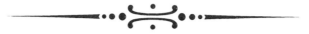

HOUSEHOLD SALVATION

There was a certain man in Caesarea called Cornelius, a centurion of the band called the Italian band, a devout man, and one that feared God with all his house, which gave much alms to the people, and prayed to God alway. He saw in a vision evidently about the ninth hour of the day an angel of God coming in to him, and saying unto him, Cornelius. And when he looked on him, he was afraid, and said, What is it, Lord? And he said unto him, Thy prayers and thine alms are come up for a memorial before God .

And he shewed us how he had seen an angel in his house, which stood and said unto him, Send men to Joppa, and call for Simon, whose surname is Peter; who shall tell thee words, whereby thou and all thy house shall be saved. And as I began to speak, the Holy Ghost fell on them, as on us at the beginning (Acts 10:1-4; 11:13-15).

Then he called for a light, and sprang in, and came trembling, and fell down before Paul and Silas, and brought them out, and said, Sirs, what must I do to be saved? And they said, Believe on the Lord Jesus Christ, and thou shalt be saved, and thy house (Acts 16:29-31).

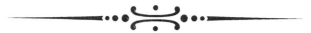

INSPIRING INSIGHTS
by Rod Parsley

I pray for the salvation of your loved ones. The Bibles declares, "You and your house shall be saved." Under the anointing of God, I join hands with you in the spirit that as you begin to call your loved ones' names before the Lord they will be saved.

I command the blinding spirit of the Antichrist to loose his hold upon your family members and your loved ones who you are believing will come into the kingdom of God. And in the spirit, I reach into the depths of hell, and pull them out in agreement with you. I declare that they are saved.

You have to be aggressive in soul winning. You can't just wish people into the kingdom of God. You have to pray them in, give them in, believe them in and speak them in. You can't let your loved ones go to hell.

What a terrible tragedy for your loved ones to go to hell. Let's do everything we can to get them into the kingdom.

❖❖❖

Today is the day for you to walk into the corridors of the doomed and damned and grapple over the souls of lost humanity. This is your battleground. This is your day.

COVENANT BLESSINGS FOR YOU AND YOUR FAMILY

MARRIAGE

And God said, Let us make man in our image, after our likeness: and let them have dominion over the fish of the sea, and over the fowl of the air, and over the cattle, and over all the earth, and over every creeping thing that creepeth upon the earth. So God created man in his own image, in the image of God created he him; male and female created he them. And God blessed them, and God said unto them, Be fruitful, and multiply, and replenish the earth, and subdue it: and have dominion over the fish of the sea, and over the fowl of the air, and over every living thing that moveth upon the earth (Genesis 1:26-28).

And the Lord God said, It is not good that the man should be alone; I will make him an help meet for him (Genesis 2:18).

Let thy fountain be blessed: and rejoice with the wife of thy youth (Proverb 5:18).

Whoso findeth a wife findeth a good thing, and obtaineth favour of the Lord (Proverb 18:22).

Marriage is a union between two imperfect individuals who, despite their imperfections, make a covenant to join their lives together, for better or for worse.

God can make your marriage exactly what you always dreamed it could be.

Marriage is a blood covenant made before the throne of God. It is a symbol of God's relationship with His church and is binding through the endless ages of eternity.

When your marriage is built on the Rock of Ages, you can endure the shaking and make it all the way. You can successfully navigate through every trial, tribulation and situation.

In your marriage, sacrifice the opportunity to be right! Say "I'm wrong!" even when you are right. Say "It's my fault!" even when it isn't. When you do, the Lord will make a dwelling place in your home, and it will be established on the right foundation.

COVENANT BLESSINGS FOR YOU AND YOUR FAMILY

PARENTS

Happy is the man that hath his quiver full of them: they shall not be ashamed, but they shall speak with the enemies in the gate (Psalm 127:5).

A good man leaveth an inheritance to his children's children: and the wealth of the sinner is laid up for the just (Proverb 13:22).

Children's children are the crown of old men; and the glory of children are their fathers (Proverb 17:6).

The just man walketh in his integrity: his children are blessed after him (Proverb 20:7).

The father of the righteous shall greatly rejoice: and he that begetteth a wise child shall have joy of him (Proverb 23:24).

INSPIRING INSIGHTS
by Rod Parsley

Parents, teach your children to respect authority. In the midst of the constant violence and pessimism of television and the movies, let them see their authority figures doing the things of God in their lives.

❖❖❖

God is looking for men who will be standard bearers and raise the standard in their homes and in their own spiritual lives.

❖❖❖

Our responsibility as parents is to find our children's God-given gifts, talents and abilities and enhance those, regardless of whether it is what we like or not. Children are a gift from God; they are not our property. Daily we should delight in the creation He has allowed us to bring into this earth. Each child is unlike any other one that has ever walked on this planet.

You have the responsibility to have a plan, to protect and to provide for your children.

Don't tell your children God will honor His Word if you will not honor your word.

COVENANT BLESSINGS FOR
YOU AND YOUR FAMILY

BEING SINGLE

But I would have you without carefulness. He that is unmarried careth for the things that belong to the Lord, how he may please the Lord: But he that is married careth for the things that are of the world, how he may please his wife.

There is difference also between a wife and a virgin. The unmarried woman careth for the things of the Lord, that she may be holy both in body and in spirit: but she that is married careth for the things of the world, how she may please her husband.

And this I speak for your own profit; not that I may cast a snare upon you, but for that which is comely, and that ye may attend upon the Lord without distraction (1 Corinthians 7:32-35).

Not that I speak in respect of want: for I have learned, in whatsoever state I am, therewith to be content. I know both how to be abased, and I know how to abound: every where and in all things I am instructed both to be full and to be hungry, both to abound and to suffer need. I can do all things through Christ which strengtheneth me (Philippians 4:11-13).

INSPIRING INSIGHTS
by Rod Parsley

In order to be complete as a married person, you must be complete as a single person—loving Jesus with all of your heart.

Being single is the greatest time in your life to work for God.

Keep your focus on the Lord and get a relationship with Him, because if God sends you a mate, then you will have something to give to that relationship. You will be a balanced and secure person. You will have stability and foundation.

Never allow the devil to tell you that you are less of a person because you are single. Allow this time to be the greatest opportunity to serve God with your whole heart, mind and strength.

The Lord wants to use you now to touch people's lives. If you allow Him, being single can be one of the best times of your life in God.

COVENANT
BLESSINGS
of
God's Provision

COVENANT BLESSINGS OF GOD'S PROVISION

ABUNDANCE

Honour the Lord with thy substance, and with the firstfruits of all thine increase: so shall thy barns be filled with plenty, and thy presses shall burst out with new wine (Proverb 3:9,10).

Bring ye all the tithes into the storehouse, that there may be meat in mine house, and prove me now herewith, saith the LORD of hosts, if I will not open you the windows of heaven, and pour you out a blessing, that there shall not be room enough to receive it. And I will rebuke the devourer for your sakes, and he shall not destroy the fruits of your ground; neither shall your vine cast her fruit before the time in the field, saith the Lord of hosts. And all nations shall call you blessed: for ye shall be a delightsome land, saith the Lord of hosts (Malachi 3:10-12).

But my God shall supply all your need according to his riches in glory by Christ Jesus (Philippians 4:19).

INSPIRING INSIGHTS
by Rod Parsley

The tithe is ten percent of the sanctified gross income and an offering is anything above it. (Genesis 28:22.)

Before you can receive what is in God's hand, you first have to unclench your fist, and offer the Lord what is in your hand.

If you want to experience God's abundance, find a church where their swords are not just being polished, but is dripping with the blood of the enemy.

Far too often, we keep the best for ourselves and offer to the Lord that which costs us little. Five percent is not ten percent. Give your best to God, and prepare to see His abundance released into your life.

God wants you to walk in abundance more than you want to be there! His mark is one of abundance. His measuring gauge always reads "full."

COVENANT BLESSINGS OF
GOD'S PROVISION

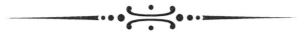

BLESSING

Behold, how good and how pleasant it is for brethren to dwell together in unity! As the dew of Hermon, and as the dew that descended upon the mountains of Zion: for there the Lord commanded the blessing, even life for evermore (Psalm 133:1,3).

The blessing of the Lord, it maketh rich, and he addeth no sorrow with it (Proverbs 10:22).

Christ hath redeemed us from the curse of the law, being made a curse for us: for it is written, Cursed is every one that hangeth on a tree: that the blessing of Abraham might come on the Gentiles through Jesus Christ; that we might receive the promise of the Spirit through faith (Galatians 3:13,14).

Blessed be the God and Father of our Lord Jesus Christ, who hath blessed us with all spiritual blessings in heavenly places in Christ (Ephesians 1:3).

We not only need "a" blessing, but also we need "the" blessing. It is time we stop settling for the status quo and receive God's best.

Throughout the ages, God has been searching for men and women in order to bless them. He took people such as Abraham, Jacob and Moses from the depths of destruction and despair—when the world had labeled them hopeless and helpless—and brought them to sit and eat at His table. He will do the same for you.

God has provided for you a life without lack—a life where He commands such a blessing that it overtakes and overshadows every problem, every fear and every trial.

For you to shun away from the blessing of God, the love of God, the mercy of God and the grace of God is for you to deny God to be who He said He is.

God didn't create you because He needed somebody to judge. He created you because He wanted somebody to love and bless.

COVENANT BLESSINGS OF GOD'S PROVISION

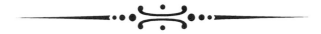

INHERITANCE

For such as be blessed of him shall inherit the earth; and they that be cursed of him shall be cut off (Psalm 37:22).

Son, thou art ever with me, and all that I have is thine (Luke 15:31).

Wherefore I also, after I heard of your faith in the Lord Jesus, and love unto all the saints, cease not to give thanks for you, making mention of you in my prayers; that the God of our Lord Jesus Christ, the Father of glory, may give unto you the spirit of wisdom and revelation in the knowledge of him: the eyes of your understanding being enlightened; that ye may know what is the hope of his calling, and what the riches of the glory of his inheritance in the saints (Ephesians 1:15-18).

Giving thanks unto the Father, which hath made us meet to be partakers of the inheritance of the saints in light (Colossians 1:12).

The restoration of your inheritance is not based on compromise, contingency or predetermined conditions of works. Rather, you are a child with a royal bloodline and an heir through Jesus Christ.

You were created for a kingly position, called for a royal purpose and crowned with a covenant promise! You are destined to dine at the King's table and to receive your rightful inheritance.

If we are heirs with Jesus Christ, then the covenant God made with Him has already provided our inheritance—or harvest! All we must do is claim it!

As a Christian, God has given you a royal robe and the family ring, marking you as one of His children; and given you the family name, signifying your right to the family inheritance! You don't have to live on crumbs!

There is no better position in life than to be a child of God.

COVENANT BLESSINGS OF GOD'S PROVISION

PROMOTION

For promotion cometh neither from the east, nor from the west, nor from the south. But God is the judge: he putteth down one, and setteth up another (Psalm 75:6,7).

Exalt her [wisdom], and she shall promote thee: she shall bring thee to honour, when thou dost embrace her (Proverb 4:7,8).

And whosoever shall exalt himself shall be abased; and he that shall humble himself shall be exalted (Matthew 23:11,12).

I'll call nobodies and make them somebodies; I'll call the unloved and make them beloved. In the place where they yelled out, 'You're nobody!' they're calling you 'God's living children' (Romans 9:25,26 The Message).

Humble yourselves therefore under the mighty hand of God, that he may exalt you in due time (1 Peter 5:6).

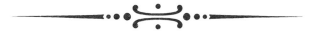

If we look to man to promote us, God never will. If we look to God to promote us, man has no choice.

In Christ you are at the Father's right hand—the seat of honor. All you want to do is serve Him. Then you know the truth. He seats you at His table for one purpose—to serve you.

The devil will lie to you about who you are. Like Mephibosheth, he will proclaim that you are ex-royalty, an ex-wife, an ex-husband or an ex-athlete. But God will raise you to regal rank, courtly companionship and a princely position.

God is in the promotion business. With Joseph, he went from the pit to Potiphar's house and then to the prison . . . but then he became the chief over all the land.

Oppression and persecution are often the opportunity for promotion.

COVENANT BLESSINGS OF
GOD'S PROVISION

PROSPERITY

But thou shalt remember the Lord thy God: for it is he that giveth thee power to get wealth, that he may establish his covenant which he sware unto thy fathers, as it is this day (Deuteronomy 8:18).

Believe in the Lord your God, so shall ye be established; believe his prophets, so shall ye prosper (2 Chronicles 20:20).

If they obey and serve him, they shall spend their days in prosperity, and their years in pleasures (Job 36:11).

Let the Lord be magnified, which hath pleasure in the prosperity of his servant (Psalm 35:27).

Beloved, I wish above all things that thou mayest prosper and be in health, even as thy soul prospereth (3 John 2).

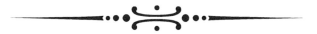

When you tithe, you are not just placing paper in a plate. You are returning something to God as an act of faith and worship. When God touches that little piece of paper He can multiply it until a mountain of obligations disappear.

God leaps off his throne and dances all over heaven at the thought of the prosperity of His people.

Prosperity is the abundant supply of God to accomplish His call upon and in your life.

Prosperity is not for our pleasure, it is our responsibility. If we don't tithe and give offerings, then we are unable to finance the end time harvest of souls.

The Bible tells us that in the last days it is going to get horrific—it will take a bag of gold to buy a piece of bread. Let the economies collapse; if it takes a bag of gold to buy a slice of bread, we will own the bakery.

COVENANT BLESSINGS OF GOD'S PROVISION

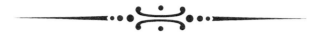

PROVISION

I have been young, and now am old; yet have I not seen the righteous forsaken, nor his seed begging bread (Psalm 37:25).

Give, and it shall be given unto you; good measure, pressed down, and shaken together, and running over, shall men give into your bosom. For with the same measure that ye mete withal it shall be measured to you again (Luke 6:38).

Fear not, little flock; for it is your Father's good pleasure to give you the kingdom (Luke 12:32).

He that spared not his own Son . . . how shall he not with him also freely give us all things (Romans 8:32).

I have planted, Apollos watered; but God gave the increase. So then neither is he that planteth any thing, neither he that watereth; but God that giveth the increase (1 Corinthians 3:6,7).

INSPIRING INSIGHTS
by Rod Parsley

You serve a God who supplies before there is a need. You don't have to wait for a blessing. He has already anointed your head with oil.

When you have done all God requires, you must then wait patiently for His provision.

God can do so much with so little—a little boy's lunch; a cloud the size of a man's hand; a borrowed stable and manger. Like your seed, they may not look like much . . . but when you release what is in your hand toward God, regardless of how seemingly insignificant, He will multiply it so your every need will be met.

You can lose everything you have, but you can never lose everything God has.

If you need something today that you didn't have yesterday, then you must do something differently today than you were doing yesterday.

The world will try to make you go to the back of the bus, but God owns the bus line, and you can sit where you please!

COVENANT BLESSINGS OF
GOD'S PROVISION

RESTORATION

Be glad then, ye children of Zion, and rejoice in the Lord your God: for he hath given you the former rain moderately, and he will cause to come down for you the rain, the former rain, and the latter rain in the first month. And I will restore to you the years that the locust hath eaten, the cankerworm, and the caterpiller, and the palmerworm, my great army which I sent among you. And ye shall eat in plenty, and be satisfied, and praise the name of the Lord your God, that hath dealt wondrously with you: and my people shall never be ashamed (Joel 2:23,25,26).

Repent ye therefore, and be converted, that your sins may be blotted out, when the times of refreshing shall come from the presence of the Lord; and he shall send Jesus Christ, which before was preached unto you: whom the heaven must receive until the times of restitution of all things, which God hath spoken by the mouth of all his holy prophets since the world began (Acts 3:19-21).

Before Jesus returns, He will restore to the body of Christ our giftings, anointing, ministry and anything else we need to pull in the net of lost souls.

God is a restorer. He will help you find things and put things back where they used to be. He wants to help you discover some misplaced treasures and recover everything the devil has stolen.

We are not going to leave this earth deprived and full of debt! As the Egyptians gave to the Israelites, the world is going to heap on us so much wealth that we are going to be able to dig ourselves out of debt and have money left over to preach the Gospel.

That thing that has destroyed, stolen and taken from you didn't just walk in one day and do it. It was the diabolical plan of your adversary. Though the devil has a plan to take you out, God has a plan to keep you in.

COVENANT BLESSINGS OF GOD'S PROVISION

SOWING & REAPING YOUR HARVEST

Behold, the days come, saith the Lord, that the plowman shall overtake the reaper, and the treader of grapes him that soweth seed; and the mountains shall drop sweet wine, and all the hills shall melt (Amos 9:13).

And he said, So is the kingdom of God, as if a man should cast seed into the ground; and should sleep, and rise night and day, and the seed should spring and grow up, he knoweth not how. For the earth bringeth forth fruit of herself; first the blade, then the ear, after that the full corn in the ear. But when the fruit is brought forth, immediately he putteth in the sickle, because the harvest is come (Mark 4:26-29).

Now he that ministereth seed to the sower both minister bread for your food, and multiply your seed sown, and increase the fruits of your righteousness (2 Corinthians 9:10).

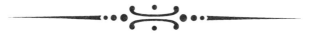

Time, as we know it, is shrinking. The days are being fulfilled when the plowman will overtake the reaper. No longer will you have to wait years, months or even weeks to reap your harvest.

You are a part of the harvest generation. It is time for you to receive a perpetual harvest.

The way to reap your miracle is to send forth your angels and speak the Word to get your harvest.

If what is in your hand is too small to be your harvest, then it must be your seed. The seed that leaves your hand will never leave your life. God will multiply it as He said.

In your hand lies the key to receiving the greatest miracle in your life. God has already scheduled your harvest, but it is up to you to start the process by sowing a seed!

COVENANT
BLESSINGS
When Facing
Life's Storms

COVENANT BLESSINGS WHEN
FACING LIFE'S STORMS

ADVERSITY

I will be glad and rejoice in thy mercy: for thou hast considered my trouble; thou hast known my soul in adversities; and hast not shut me up into the hand of the enemy: thou hast set my feet in a large room (Psalm 31:7,8).

Blessed is the man whom thou chastenest, O Lord, and teachest him out of thy law; that thou mayest give him rest from the days of adversity, until the pit be digged for the wicked. For the Lord will not cast off his people, neither will he forsake his inheritance (Psalm 94:12-14).

For which cause we faint not; but though our outward man perish, yet the inward man is renewed day by day. For our light affliction, which is but for a moment, worketh for us a far more exceeding and eternal weight of glory; While we look not at the things which are seen, but at the things which are not seen: for the things which are seen are temporal; but the things which are not seen are eternal (2 Corinthians 4:16-18).

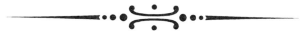

When you know the strategies of Satan he cannot take you by surprise. When you know there is a spiritual war going on, you will not be vulnerable to the attack of the enemy.

Throughout history men and women whose destinies should have been sealed by defeat, discouragement and disappointment have confounded their critics. They have astonished their adversaries and staggered so-called friends and family as they stood valiantly in the victory born in the very crucible of conflict. They were conflicts designed to cause their ultimate demise.

Held in high regard only among the excommunicated, eccentric and extreme, these exiles of society hoped against hope, believed beyond belief, and refused to flinch in the face of adversity in order to accomplish their aspirations.

When you stop waiting on the spectacular and look to the supernatural, you'll begin to rejoice in the middle of adversity.

Look through the window of adversity and on to the blood that saves, sets free and delivers!

COVENANT BLESSINGS WHEN FACING LIFE'S STORMS

BROKEN HEART

The Lord is nigh unto them that are of a broken heart; and saveth such as be of a contrite spirit (Psalm 34:18).

The sacrifices of God are a broken spirit: a broken and a contrite heart, O God, thou wilt not despise (Psalm 51:17).

He healeth the broken in heart, and bindeth up their wounds. He telleth the number of the stars; he calleth them all by their names. Great is our Lord, and of great power: his understanding is infinite (Psalm 147:3-5).

The Spirit of the Lord God is upon me; because the Lord hath anointed me to preach good tidings unto the meek; he hath sent me to bind up the brokenhearted, to proclaim liberty to the captives, and the opening of the prison to them that are bound; to proclaim the acceptable year of the Lord, and the day of vengeance of our God; to comfort all that mourn (Isaiah 61:1,2).

Jesus is strong enough to defeat devils, yet gentle enough to lay His mighty hand upon you and heal your broken heart.

As the light appeared at the end of the cold, dark tomb, with nail-pierced hands Jesus lifted the gates of death and hell off their rusty hinges. He flung them into the blackened abyss of eternity and went wading through the ashes of bygone millenniums wherein are broken dreams, broken lives and broken hearts.

Jesus was on a rescue mission to retrieve you from the clutches of Satan.

The blood of Jesus is like the balm of Gilead for the brokenhearted. Reach out and receive the touch of the Master's hand.

God not only wants to mend your broken heart, but also He wants to give you a new heart. He wants you to forget the wounds of your past, and receive a brand new future full of expectation and life in Him.

COVENANT BLESSINGS WHEN FACING LIFE'S STORMS

PERSECUTION

Blessed are they which are persecuted for righteousness' sake: for theirs is the kingdom of heaven. Blessed are ye, when men shall revile you, and persecute you, and shall say all manner of evil against you falsely, for my sake. Rejoice, and be exceeding glad: for great is your reward in heaven: for so persecuted they the prophets which were before you (Matthew 5:10-12).

But we have this treasure in earthen vessels, that the excellency of the power may be of God, and not of us. We are troubled on every side, yet not distressed; we are perplexed, but not in despair; persecuted, but not forsaken; cast down, but not destroyed; always bearing about in the body the dying of the Lord Jesus, that the life also of Jesus might be made manifest in our body. For we which live are alway delivered unto death for Jesus' sake, that the life also of Jesus might be made manifest in our mortal flesh (2 Corinthians 4:7-11).

Yea, and all that will live godly in Christ Jesus shall suffer persecution (2 Timothy 3:12).

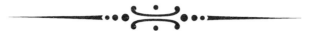

INSPIRING INSIGHTS
by Rod Parsley

Faith is gained from recounting your persecution. However, you cannot recount your persecution unless, alongside of it, you begin to think about your deliverance.

Persecution is often the chance for God to take you to another level of glory. Joseph would have never made it to the palace had he not taken a pit stop in the prison.

Satan likes to persecute certain Christians (Acts 12:1). I want to be one of those Christians, because persecution is a stepping stone into the presence of God.

Persecution keeps you sober and vigilant. Persecution keeps the fires burning.

Something happens to your life when you become a stranger to persecution and tribulation. It is then that you become a stranger to the presence of God. When this happens you begin to develop a humanistic self-sufficiency, that "I'm all right" attitude.

SUFFERING

For I reckon that the sufferings of this present time are not worthy to be compared with the glory which shall be revealed in us (Romans 8:18).

Yea doubtless, and I count all things but loss for the excellency of the knowledge of Christ Jesus my Lord: for whom I have suffered the loss of all things, and do count them but dung, that I may win Christ, and be found in him, not having mine own righteousness, which is of the law, but that which is through the faith of Christ, the righteousness which is of God by faith: That I may know him, and the power of his resurrection, and the fellowship of his sufferings, being made conformable unto his death; If by any means I might attain unto the resurrection of the dead (Philippians 3:8-11).

It is a faithful saying: for if we be dead with him, we shall also live with him: if we suffer, we shall also reign with him: if we deny him, he also will deny us (2 Timothy 2:11,12).

There is a glory in suffering that many in the body of Christ have yet to be willing to enter into. It is not sickness and disease, for that was dealt with at Calvary.

God is wanting to use you to prove to this world He has power to take you through any storm that life can present to you.

❖❖❖

Jesus suffered once and for all nailing our sin and sickness to His cross. There's no need for you to suffer under the penalty of sin and death any longer. The law of life in Christ Jesus can make you free from the law of sin and death!

❖❖❖

It is a great honor to suffer with Christ, because one day we will receive a far greater reward in glory. We are being changed from glory to glory.

The suffering of the Lord which we are to identify with is this—we cannot get to enough people with enough power to proclaim the Gospel message fast enough before the coming of the Lord.

COVENANT BLESSINGS WHEN FACING LIFE'S STORMS

TRIALS

O bless our God, ye people, and make the voice of his praise to be heard: which holdeth our soul in life, and suffereth not our feet to be moved. For thou, O God, hast proved us: thou hast tried us, as silver is tried (Psalm 66:8-10).

Wherein ye greatly rejoice, though now for a season, if need be, ye are in heaviness through manifold temptations: That the trial of your faith, being much more precious than of gold that perisheth, though it be tried with fire, might be found unto praise and honour and glory at the appearing of Jesus Christ (1 Peter 1:6,7).

Beloved, think it not strange concerning the fiery trial which is to try you, as though some strange thing happened unto you: but rejoice, inasmuch as ye are partakers of Christ's sufferings; that, when his glory shall be revealed, ye may be glad also with exceeding joy (1 Peter 4:12,13).

When the trials of your faith come and you feel like bowing down under their weight, remember the three Hebrew children and the fiery furnace. They did not bow, and they did not burn.

The devil would like you to settle for less than God's best. He always has a consolation prize. But you need to plant your feet and say, "I refuse to be refused, and I deny to be denied!"

What an opportunity! God wants to turn your problem into a project!

God wants to turn your trial into a mighty, manifested miracle testimony of His very own delivering power.

The flames of peril, persecution, people, trouble, trial, temptation and tribulation will be yours! Make no mistake. Do not think it strange concerning the fiery trial which is to try your faith. Understand in that hour God is burning permanence into you. God is burning "stick-to-itiveness" into you!

COVENANT BLESSINGS WHEN FACING LIFE'S STORMS

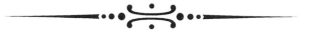

TRIBULATION

These things I have spoken unto you, that in me ye might have peace. In the world ye shall have tribulation: but be of good cheer; I have overcome the world (John 16:33).

And when they had preached the gospel to that city, and had taught many, they returned again to Lystra, and to Iconium, and Antioch, confirming the souls of the disciples, and exhorting them to continue in the faith, and that we must through much tribulation enter into the kingdom of God (Acts 14:21,22).

Therefore being justified by faith, we have peace with God through our Lord Jesus Christ: by whom also we have access by faith into this grace wherein we stand, and rejoice in hope of the glory of God. And not only so, but we glory in tribulations also: knowing that tribulation worketh patience; and patience, experience; and experience, hope: And hope maketh not ashamed; because the love of God is shed abroad in our hearts by the Holy Ghost which is given unto us (Romans 5:1-5).

What is happening in you is greater than what is happening to you.

To God, your dark tomb of tribulation is just the fertile ground from which He will resurrect your deliverance.

When you begin to view the tribulations that are coming your way as either being from the will of God, or at least being allowed to come into your life by the Spirit of God, it is then you will learn to love the cross. When you learn to love the cross, you're dangerous to the devil; because it's at the cross we give ourselves to God and God gives Himself to us.

Like Daniel, the devil may throw us into the lion's den; however, we'll reckon our position, turn our face to Jerusalem, offer our prayer to God, pillow our head in the shaggy mane of the lion, and sleep like a baby all night. Our God is able to deliver us!

If you want to get the world's attention, allow God to turn your tribulation into triumph!

COVENANT BLESSINGS WHEN FACING LIFE'S STORMS

TROUBLE

This poor man cried, and the Lord heard him, and saved him out of all his troubles (Psalm 34:6).

The righteous cry, and the Lord heareth, and delivereth them out of all their troubles (Psalm 34:17).

O Lord, be gracious unto us; we have waited for thee: be thou their arm every morning, our salvation also in the time of trouble (Isaiah 33:2).

The Lord is good, a strong-hold in the day of trouble; and he knoweth them that trust in him. But with an overrunning flood he will make an utter end of the place thereof, and darkness shall pursue his enemies (Nahum 1:7,8).

Who comforteth us in all our tribulation, that we may be able to comfort them which are in any trouble, by the comfort wherewith we ourselves are comforted of God (2 Corinthians 1:4).

INSPIRING INSIGHTS
by Rod Parsley

The Gospel we have comes with trouble, because it's only in our trouble we find out who He is.

God allows you to get in trouble, but you must understand He doesn't think like you do. He didn't get you in trouble to leave you there. He is ready to bring you out.

The only reason He lets you fall into trouble is to bear His right arm, flex His muscle, and bring you out on the other side!

You should shout when you have trouble, because God counted you worthy to walk through it and bear His name and mark. You will come out on the other side dancing on the head of your defeated adversary. At the same time, give all the glory to the God who delivered you from the devil, because you couldn't do it yourself!

God wants to turn your tribulation into triumph and your trial into a testimony. What can the devil do with you when he knows you will never quit?!

COVENANT BLESSINGS WHEN
FACING LIFE'S STORMS

WORRY

Fret not thyself because of evildoers, neither be thou envious against the workers of iniquity. For they shall soon be cut down like the grass, and wither as the green herb. Trust in the Lord, and do good; so shalt thou dwell in the land, and verily thou shalt be fed. Delight thyself also in the Lord; and he shall give thee the desires of thine heart.

Commit thy way unto the Lord; trust also in him; and he shall bring it to pass. And he shall bring forth thy righteousness as the light, and thy judgment as the noonday. Rest in the Lord, and wait patiently for him: fret not thyself because of him who prospereth in his way, because of the man who bringeth wicked devices to pass. Cease from anger, and forsake wrath: fret not thyself in any wise to do evil. For evildoers shall be cut off: but those that wait upon the Lord, they shall inherit the earth (Psalm 37:1-9).

Fret not thyself because of evil men, neither be thou envious at the wicked; for there shall be no reward to the evil man; the candle of the wicked shall be put out (Proverb 24:19,20).

Let the storms rage high. Let the dark clouds rise. Don't be worried for you are sheltered safe within the arms of God, and nothing shall harm you!

Worry is an insult to God. It says you don't believe He is going to take care of you. It says you don't believe God is God and not a man that He should lie.

Each one of us can testify we have never been in a fire that God wasn't already there when we showed up. We have never been in a flood that He wasn't already in before we arrived.

No matter how much you worry today, you are not able to change any of your circumstances. You are not going to put any more finances in your bank account. So instead of doing what won't work, find out what will work—that is, confessing the Word of God.

Do something differently today than you did yesterday, so you can have tomorrow what you don't have today!

COVENANT BLESSINGS
In Times Of. . .

CONFUSION

In thee, O Lord, do I put my trust: let me never be put to confusion (Psalm 71:1).

For the Lord God will help me; therefore shall I not be confounded: therefore have I set my face like a flint, and I know that I shall not be ashamed. He is near that justifieth me; who will contend with me? Let us stand together: who is mine adversary? Let him come near to me. (Isaiah 50:7,8).

For God is not the author of confusion, but of peace, as in all churches of the saints (1 Corinthians 14:33).

Ye also, as lively stones, are built up a spiritual house, an holy priesthood, to offer up spiritual sacrifices, acceptable to God by Jesus Christ. Wherefore also it is contained in the scripture, Behold, I lay in Sion a chief corner stone, elect, precious: and he that believeth on him shall not be confounded (1 Peter 2:5,6).

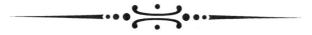

The devil is the author of confusion, but your Father has a plan for you!

The directive of God always flows in rivers of peace. He does not operate in confusion, but rather He operates in peace.

You may say, "Well, what should I do?" Do what you're doing. Oftentimes struggles come because you want to move ahead of God. But Psalm 37:23 says, "The steps of a good man are ordered by the Lord." He doesn't make the race known to you, only the steps. He is Alpha and Omega. He lets you know the beginning and the end, but often He's not real clear about the "in between," because He wants you to walk in faith.

❖❖❖

When confusion tries to bombard your mind, take authority by saying, "I take hold of confusion and I extract it from my mind. I command clarity of thought to come to me and singleness of purpose. I command peace to flood my mind—the peace that passes understanding, even in the middle of tragedy and trial. I have the mind of Christ. The peace of God and the security of the communion of the Holy Ghost come to me now!"

COVENANT BLESSINGS
IN TIMES OF...

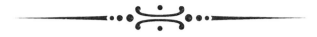

CONDEMNATION

The wicked watcheth the righteous, and seeketh to slay him. The Lord will not leave him in his hand, nor condemn him when he is judged (Psalm 37:32,33).

He that justifieth the wicked, and he that condemneth the just, even they both are abomination to the Lord (Proverb 17:15).

For God so loved the world, that he gave his only begotten Son, that whosoever believeth in him should not perish, but have everlasting life. For God sent not his Son into the world to condemn the world; but that the world through him might be saved (John 3:16,17).

There is therefore now no condemnation to them which are in Christ Jesus, who walk not after the flesh, but after the Spirit. For the law of the Spirit of life in Christ Jesus hath made me free from the law of sin and death (Romans 8:1,2).

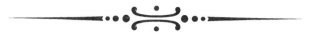

God is far bigger than your ability to please Him—He loves you for who you are.

The difference between condemnation and conviction is that condemnation will tell you to go into a room that is in complete disarray. The furniture is destroyed and turned upside down. The drawers are pulled out and everything is dumped on the floor. The lights are off and it is completely pitch black; and God says,"Go in the room and straighten it up." That's condemnation.

With conviction the room is the same, God is the same and you are the same. But God turns the light on and then tells you to straighten the room up. That's conviction.

Conviction is to your spirit what pain is to your body. Without pain you could walk down a sandy beach, step on a broken bottle, slit your foot open and bleed to death. Pain is not your enemy but, rather, an indication one exists.

So it is with conviction the Holy Spirit prompts, corrects and brings us into alignment with the perfect will of God. Why? So we don't die, and we can manifest the very glory of the living God in the midst of a sin-cursed world.

COVENANT BLESSINGS IN TIMES OF. . .

DISTRESS

In my distress I called upon the Lord, and cried to my God: and he did hear my voice out of his temple, and my cry did enter into his ears (2 Samuel 22:7).

Let the redeemed of the Lord say so, whom he hath redeemed from the hand of the enemy; and gathered them out of the lands, from the east, and from the west, from the north, and from the south. They wandered in the wilderness in a solitary way; they found no city to dwell in. Hungry and thirsty, their soul fainted in them. Then they cried unto the Lord in their trouble, and he delivered them out of their distresses (Psalm 107:2-6).

In my distress I cried unto the Lord, and he heard me (Psalm 120:1).

For thou hast been a strength to the poor, a strength to the needy in his distress, a refuge from the storm, a shadow from the heat, when the blast of the terrible ones is as a storm against the wall (Isaiah 25:4).

Spiritual perspiration is a good indication you are making some advancement toward the prize that is laid before you. When the hurdles of despair and distress come upon you, know this: God has never called you to do anything He has not already equipped you to accomplish.

If you are going to serve God you are going to have distress. It is just that you don't have to be defeated. You don't have to lose. You don't have to stay down. You are on the winning side!

You've crossed Calvary's bridge. You've come all the way across the chasm. You've made it into the kingdom of God. You are not in the kingdom of darkness; you're in the kingdom of light. You're not in the kingdom of distress; you're in the kingdom of deliverance. You're not in the kingdom of chaos; you're in the kingdom of Christ. You're here. You have made it!

Evil days produce opportunity for kingdom enterprise. If there was ever an hour where the church should stand up and declare, "He will comfort you" to those in distress, it is now.

COVENANT BLESSINGS
IN TIMES OF...

FEAR

The Lord is my light and my salvation; whom shall I fear? The Lord is the strength of my life; of whom shall I be afraid (Psalm 27:1)?

Fear thou not; for I am with thee: be not dismayed; for I am thy God: I will strengthen thee; yea, I will help thee; yea, I will uphold thee with the right hand of my righteousness (Isaiah 41:10).

For God hath not given us the spirit of fear; but of power, and of love, and of a sound mind (2 Timothy 1:7).

For he hath said, I will never leave thee, nor forsake thee. So that we may boldly say, The Lord is my helper, and I will not fear what man shall do unto me (Hebrews 13:5,6).

There is no fear in love; but perfect love casteth out fear: because fear hath torment. He that feareth is not made perfect in love (1 John 4:18).

Fear is False Evidence Appearing Real. It is an illusion. God commands us to be full of faith and not fear.

Fear will lead you to "hide out" away from the grace and provision of God. Some hide out behind an abusive relationship. For others, it may be work, alcohol or drugs. Still others crawl into the secret and dark world of their computers. They become someone they are not, in order to satisfy a hidden craving.

Lost in a seemingly endless cycle of sin, with no exit sign in sight, many settle in their circumstances, believing there is no way out. Pleasure turns to pain and success turns into shame. They settle for the crumbs that fall from the table instead of pulling their chair up beside the King of Kings and Lord of Lords who has freely given them all things.

❖❖❖

Do not obey God out of an obligation to a written ordinance, through a spirit of fear. Obey Him out of the workings of His spirit on the inside of you, where your sole desire is to let His kingdom come into your life.

GRIEF

Who hath believed our report? And to whom is the arm of the Lord revealed? For he shall grow up before him as a tender plant, and as a root out of a dry ground: he hath no form nor comeliness; and when we shall see him, there is no beauty that we should desire him. He is despised and rejected of men; a man of sorrows, and acquainted with grief: and we hid as it were our faces from him; he was despised, and we esteemed him not. Surely he hath borne our griefs, and carried our sorrows: yet we did esteem him stricken, smitten of God, and afflicted (Isaiah 53:1-4).

For the Lord will not cast off for ever: For he doth not afflict willingly nor grieve the children of men (Lamentations 3:31,33).

For this is thankworthy, if a man for conscience toward God endure grief, suffering wrongfully. For what glory is it, if, when ye be buffeted for your faults, ye shall take it patiently? but if, when ye do well, and suffer for it, ye take it patiently, this is acceptable with God (1 Peter 2:19,20).

INSPIRING INSIGHTS
by Rod Parsley

When you are overwhelmed with grief at the loss of a loved one, remember your grief is outstripped by the hope which remains. Though that person has passed away, yet shall they live. That's our hope.

When sorrow all around closes in, when darkness buffets you on every side and when every devil in hell seems to have only your name in their Rolodex—know your hour of deliverance has come!

Your grief touches God, and you can't touch Him without being touched by Him.

The words to the following song have so touched my heart in my greatest hours of need, "In seasons of distress and grief, my soul has often found relief; and oft escaped the tempter's snare by thy return sweet hour of prayer."

God knows your tomorrow's like you know your yesterday's, and He has already prepared a haven of hope for your hour of sorrow and grief. He has not been caught off guard but is, rather, waiting to comfort you!

COVENANT BLESSINGS IN TIMES OF...

SORROW

Therefore the redeemed of the Lord shall return, and come with singing unto Zion; and everlasting joy shall be upon their head: they shall obtain gladness and joy; and sorrow and mourning shall flee away (Isaiah 51:11).

Therefore they shall come and sing in the height of Zion, and shall flow together to the goodness of the Lord, for wheat, and for wine, and for oil, and for the young of the flock and of the herd: and their soul shall be as a watered garden; and they shall not sorrow any more at all (Jeremiah 31:12).

And ye now therefore have sorrow: but I will see you again, and your heart shall rejoice, and your joy no man taketh from you (John 16:22).

For godly sorrow worketh repentance to salvation not to be repented of: but the sorrow of the world worketh death (2 Corinthians 7:10).

INSPIRING INSIGHTS
by Rod Parsley

Do you know what sorrow is? It is the joy factor in your life. Death is the only seedbed of life. Jesus says, "If you want to live you will have to die. And when you die you will live. Share with me in my death and, you will share with me in my resurrection from the dead." (Philippians 3:10,11.)

If you are going to have revival and feel victory, then you are going to drink a cup of sorrow. If you want to bear witness of Jesus, the world will not be impressed with your words.

What will get the world's attention is when you are thrown into the same prison with them, and instead of complaining, you do as Paul and Silas did in Acts chapter 16. When you begin to raise your hands and sing praises unto God, the world will notice there is something different about you. If you want to get the world's attention, turn your problems into praise.

❖❖❖

One glimpse of Jesus' dear face and all sorrow will be erased! It will be worth it all when we see Him!

COVENANT BLESSINGS
IN TIMES OF...

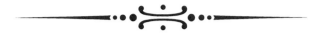

TEMPTATION

There hath no temptation taken you but such as is common to man: but God is faithful, who will not suffer you to be tempted above that ye are able; but will with the temptation also make a way to escape, that ye may be able to bear it (1 Corinthians 10:13).

For we have not an high priest which cannot be touched with the feeling of our infirmities; but was in all points tempted like as we are, yet without sin. Let us therefore come boldly unto the throne of grace, that we may obtain mercy, and find grace to help in time of need (Hebrews 4:15,16).

Blessed is the man that endureth temptation: for when he is tried, he shall receive the crown of life, which the Lord hath promised to them that love him (James 1:12).

The Lord knoweth how to deliver the godly out of temptations, and to reserve the unjust unto the day of judgment to be punished (2 Peter 2:9).

Temptation, when consistently repelled, disappears . . . and when habitually kept at a distance, ceases to exist.

When Satan tries to seduce you through a multitude of temptations you can look him square in the eye and say, "I am the righteousness of God. I am created in Christ Jesus unto good works. I don't have to sin. I don't have to cower to you. I don't have to bend in defeat. I don't have to bow! I can stand with my backbone like a T-rail and say, 'Greater is He that is in me than he that is in the world'" (1 John 4:4). That's our covenant blessing as a child of God!

Every believer who is baptized in Holy Ghost power has resident within them all the power necessary to overcome every sin, temptation and evil habit.

When temptation rises against you, instead of running toward it, run toward the anointing of God that is available to break the back of that temptation in your life!

COVENANT BLESSINGS
IN TIMES OF. . .

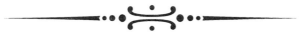

WEAKNESS

Behold, thou hast instructed many, and thou hast strengthened the weak hands. Thy words have upholden him that was falling, and thou hast strengthened the feeble knees (Job 4:3,4).

Beat your plowshares into swords, and your pruninghooks into spears: let the weak say, I am strong (Joel 3:10).

But God hath chosen the foolish things of the world to confound the wise; and God hath chosen the weak things of the world to confound the things which are mighty (1 Corinthians 1:27).

And he said unto me, My grace is sufficient for thee: for my strength is made perfect in weakness. Most gladly therefore will I rather glory in my infirmities, that the power of Christ may rest upon me. Therefore I take pleasure in infirmities, in reproaches, in necessities, in persecutions, in distresses for Christ's sake: for when I am weak, then am I strong (2 Corinthians 12:9,10).

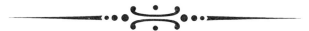

What does it take to be a great leader? You have to be weak. You have to recognize your weakness but, thank God, when you recognize your weakness, you recognize God's strength.

Let weakness lie limp on the shoulder of God, for our God is able.

The purpose of God's government in your life is to end weakness. Everything God does, all His purposes, are to end weakness—because only by struggle can strength be had. Only by attempting flight and falling can you, like an eaglet, ever learn to fly. It would be so easy to just let God leave you in the nest. You want to be comfortable, and you get mad at God when He moves you out of your comfort zone. He requires strength of you and requires you to "having done all, to stand" (Ephesians 6:13). To be removed from the conflict is certain death.

In times of weakness when you feel as though you can't go on remember: God's Word is inexhaustible. Every moutaintop reveals another mountain range.

COVENANT BLESSINGS
IN TIMES OF. . .

FEELING AFRAID

Be merciful unto me, O God: for man would swallow me up; he fighting daily oppresseth me. Mine enemies would daily swallow me up: for they be many that fight against me, O thou most High. What time I am afraid, I will trust in thee (Psalm 56:1-3).

He shall cover thee with his feathers, and under his wings shalt thou trust: his truth shall be thy shield and buckler. Thou shalt not be afraid for the terror by night; nor for the arrow that flieth by day; Nor for the pestilence that walketh in darkness; nor for the destruction that wasteth at noonday. A thousand shall fall at thy side, and ten thousand at thy right hand; but it shall not come nigh thee (Psalm 91:4-7).

When thou liest down, thou shalt not be afraid: yea, thou shalt lie down, and thy sleep shall be sweet. Be not afraid of sudden fear, neither of the desolation of the wicked, when it cometh. For the Lord shall be thy confidence, and shall keep thy foot from being taken (Proverb 3:24-26).

Don't be afraid, for the same God who delivered David from the hand of the lion and the bear is the same God who will deliver you. He will deliver you from whatever you face. Don't allow your heart to be disquieted within you; be of good courage. You will win if you faint not.

God will call you to do things you've never done before. Don't be afraid. He will call you to the front lines of battle. Stick your chin up, square your shoulders, and like a soldier of the Lord say, "I don't care what you think. I'm going to please Him who has called me to be a soldier."

Fear is the counterfeit of faith. Also, each is mutually exclusive and cancels one another out. They can't live in the same heart . . . so when you are full of faith, you cannot fear!

Don't be afraid of tomorrow or the ravaging of your adversary. Rather, keep your eyes on Jesus and see Him wearing the garments of mortal conflict. He is clothed in a vesture that's been dipped in blood, and He is ready to do battle on your behalf!

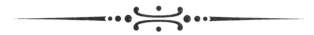

FEELING ANGRY

A wrathful man stirreth up strife: but he that is slow to anger appeaseth strife (Proverb 15:18).

He that is slow to anger is better than the mighty; and he that ruleth his spirit than he that taketh a city (Proverb 16:32).

The discretion of a man deferreth his anger; and it is his glory to pass over a transgression (Proverb 19:11).

Be ye angry, and sin not: let not the sun go down upon your wrath: Neither give place to the devil (Ephesians 4:26,27).

Let all bitterness, and wrath, and anger, and clamour, and evil speaking, be put away from you, with all malice: And be ye kind one to another, tenderhearted, forgiving one another, even as God for Christ's sake hath forgiven you (Ephesians 4:31,32).

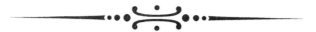

When anger tries to come upon you, you must speak to that spirit in the name of Jesus! During the moment of conflict say, "I speak to the spirit called anger, and in the name of Jesus Christ of Nazareth and by the blood of the Lamb, I rebuke you. You are not welcome in my life, and I command you to go!" Then, begin to watch supernatural joy rise on the inside of you, and you will even begin to forget why you were angry in the first place!

At times when you feel angry, you must give up your right to be right—in order to keep a continual flow of the blessings of God in your life.

Webster defines endurance as the ability to remain firm in the presence of suffering and tribulation without resorting to anger.

The devil would like nothing better than to stop God's power from flowing in your life because of a previous wrong or hurt which results in anger or bitterness. It is during these times you must remember that there is a crown laid up for the overcomer . . . and when you see Jesus face-to-face it will be worth having told the devil you wouldn't allow him to steal your reward!

COVENANT BLESSINGS
IN TIMES OF . . .

FEELING FORSAKEN

The Lord also will be a refuge for the oppressed, a refuge in times of trouble. And they that know thy name will put their trust in thee: for thou, Lord, hast not forsaken them that seek thee (Psalm 9:9,10).

When my father and my mother forsake me, then the Lord will take me up. Teach me thy way, O Lord, and lead me in a plain path, because of mine enemies (Psalm 27:10,11).

When the poor and needy seek water, and there is none, and their tongue faileth for thirst, I the Lord will hear them, I the God of Israel will not forsake them. I will open rivers in high places, and fountains in the midst of the valleys: I will make the wilderness a pool of water, and the dry land springs of water. I will plant in the wilderness the cedar, the shittah tree, and the myrtle, and the oil tree; I will set in the desert the fir tree, and the pine, and the box tree together: that they may see, and know, and consider, and understand together, that the hand of the Lord hath done this, and the Holy One of Israel hath created it (Isaiah 41:17-20).

When you feel everyone has forsaken you and there is no one to turn to, before you hit the crevices and the rocks of wreck and ruin, underneath you will find the everlasting arms of God, and He will bear you upon his wings!

Tough times don't last! Tough people do!

Each of us at times has been lonely and felt forsaken and thought we did not have a friend in the world. There has never been a time that you have drawn a breath on this people planet that you could have exclaimed what Jesus exclaimed in that very first expression, "My God, my God, why have you forsaken me?" (Mark 15:34). There has never been a moment that He has forsaken you. There has yet to be a time when He has turned His face from looking upon you!

When forsaken by friends and family while trying to live for God, it is then you need to learn to love His process. It is then you can say, "I have confidence that no matter what rises against me from the smoking corridors of the demonic underworld—I know my Redeemer liveth, and I am going to make it all the way through."

COVENANT BLESSINGS
IN TIMES OF. . .

FEELING OVERWHELMED

The Lord is my rock, and my fortress, and my deliverer; my God, my strength, in whom I will trust; my buckler, and the horn of my salvation, and my high tower. I will call upon the Lord, who is worthy to be praised: so shall I be saved from mine enemies (Psalm 18:2,3).

From the end of the earth will I cry unto thee, when my heart is overwhelmed: lead me to the rock that is higher than I. For thou hast been a shelter for me, and a strong tower from the enemy. I will abide in thy tabernacle for ever: I will trust in the covert of thy wings. Selah (Psalm 61:2-4).

When I said, My foot slippeth; thy mercy, O Lord, held me up. In the multitude of my thoughts within me thy comforts delight my soul (Psalm 94:18,19).

And Jesus looking upon them saith, With men it is impossible, but not with God: for with God all things are possible (Mark 10:27).

INSPIRING INSIGHTS
by Rod Parsley

If God leads you into a situation that seems overwhelming, you have a choice to make. You can either give up, quit and say, "Well, I can't do this, so what's the use in trying?" Or you can throw yourself upon the mercy of a good and gracious God who is more than able to bring you through every situation and circumstance.

❖❖❖

It's not wrong to be in a situation where you feel as though you are overwhelmed. However, there are choices and decisions you have to make in a situation like that—to enable the power of God to sustain you and strengthen you. God doesn't want you to quit in the middle of your situation. He wants to bring you all the way through to the very end so you can be on the winning side!

❖❖❖

Don't feel overwhelmed by your responsibilities. Recognize the Greater One lives on the inside of you, and it's He that gives you the ability to do what you feel cannot be done.

COVENANT BLESSINGS
for
God's Guidance

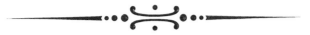
DESIRE

The king shall joy in thy strength, O Lord; and in thy salvation how greatly shall he rejoice! Thou hast given him his heart's desire, and hast not withholden the request of his lips. Selah (Psalm 21:1,2).

The eyes of all wait upon thee; and thou givest them their meat in due season. Thou openest thine hand, and satisfiest the desire of every living thing (Psalm 145:15,16).

He will fulfil the desire of them that fear him: he also will hear their cry, and will save them (Psalm 145:19).

The desire of the righteous is only good: but the expectation of the wicked is wrath (Proverb 11:23).

And if we know that he hear us, whatsoever we ask, we know that we have the petitions that we desired of him (1 John 5:15).

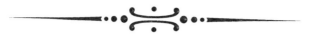

God wants to give you a significant breakthrough, that thing you have desired for so long, you have almost forgotten how much you wanted it.

The proof of desire is in your determination to pursue it. What are you pursuing? God has already made provision for you to receive the very thing you have been believing Him for.

When the desire in front of you gets bigger than the pain behind you, you are ready to give birth to a dream and a miracle!

It is time to take the limits off God and say, "Whatever you put as the desires of my heart, I'm ready to believe for them!"

Psalm 37 says God will give you the desires of your heart. This isn't speaking about good ideas. It is talking about something God issued forth over the sapphire sill of heaven's gate, and with the flaming finger of the Holy Ghost, engraved upon the fleshly tablets of your heart. They are not your desires; they are His desires.

COVENANT BLESSINGS
FOR GOD'S GUIDANCE

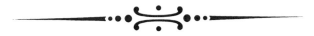

DIRECTION

Trust in the Lord with all thine heart; and lean not unto thine own understanding. In all thy ways acknowledge him, and he shall direct thy paths (Proverb 3:5,6).

The righteousness of the perfect shall direct his way: but the wicked shall fall by his own wickedness (Proverb 11:5).

A man's heart deviseth his way: but the Lord directeth his steps (Proverb 16:9).

A wicked man hardeneth his face: but as for the upright, he directeth his way (Proverb 21:29).

I have made the earth, and created man upon it: I, even my hands, have stretched out the heavens, and all their host have I commanded. I have raised him up in righteousness, and I will direct all his ways: he shall build my city, and he shall let go my captives, not for price nor reward, saith the Lord of hosts (Isaiah 45:12,13).

INSPIRING INSIGHTS
by Rod Parsley

Sometimes it is easy to feel like the clay in the hands of the Potter, spinning out of control. (Jeremiah 18:3,4.) But you must understand that the God of the clay is also the God of the wheel. It is His responsibility to shape you and to spin you until you are not going by your own direction but by His leading and prompting! It is during these times you must try to hold on! But you don't have to hold on that tight, because when you can't hold on, His hands are molding and making an impression upon your life.

I would rather be on the wheel not knowing where I was going, but knowing in whose hands I was . . . because to be off the wheel is to be out of His hands and care!

❖❖❖

If you think the direction of God is a primrose path, the easy way, you could not be further from the truth. It is rarely the easy way, but His way is definitely the better and the blessed way!

❖❖❖

God never shows you the immediate future, He only shows you the beginning and the end. The devil always wants to bring up the immediate. You have to refuse to look at the immediate but, rather, look at the end result!

COVENANT BLESSINGS
FOR GOD'S GUIDANCE

PURPOSE

Every purpose is established by counsel: and with good advice make war (Proverb 20:18).

To every thing there is a season, and a time to every purpose under the heaven (Ecclesiastes 3:1).

I, even I, have spoken; yea, I have called him: I have brought him, and he shall make his way prosperous (Isaiah 48:15).

Wherefore also we pray always for you, that our God would count you worthy of this calling, and fulfil all the good pleasure of his goodness, and the work of faith with power (2 Thessalonians 1:11)

He that committeth sin is of the devil; for the devil sinneth from the beginning. For this purpose the Son of God was manifested, that he might destroy the works of the devil (1 John 3:8).

The calling of God is a holy thing. Never take the gifts and abilities given to you by God for granted. (Romans 11:29.)

Just as a river flows on a steady course, God, your Father, has the perfect plan for you.

We serve a Sovereign God, and He is in control. He did not pay half price for you. God paid the full price, and He has a plan and a purpose for your life!

God knows who you are, and He has a predestined, divine assignment for your life. Like Joseph, His desire is to take you out of the pit and put you into the palace!

You are strategically positioned by God exactly where you are, on the road to where you need to be! Your God is a God of progression! Your God is a God of movement! Your God is a God of purpose, and that purpose is to guide you into His perfect will. You are not a mouse in a maze, but you are His child whom He takes by the hand and leads onto greater things!

COVENANT BLESSINGS
FOR GOD'S GUIDANCE

RECOGNIZING GOD'S VOICE

She [Wisdom] standeth in the top of high places, by the way in the places of the paths. She crieth at the gates, at the entry of the city, at the coming in at the doors. Unto you, O men, I call; and my voice is to the sons of man (Proverb 8:2-4).

Verily, verily, I say unto you, He that entereth not by the door into the sheepfold, but climbeth up some other way, the same is a thief and a robber. But he that entereth in by the door is the shepherd of the sheep. To him the porter openeth; and the sheep hear his voice: and he calleth his own sheep by name, and leadeth them out. And when he putteth forth his own sheep, he goeth before them, and the sheep follow him: for they know his voice. (John 10:1-4).

My sheep hear my voice, and I know them, and they follow me (John 10:27).

While it is said, To day if ye will hear his voice, harden not your hearts, as in the provocation (Hebrews 3:15).

INSPIRING INSIGHTS
by Rod Parsley

If we cannot hear the voice of God through a man of God—and respond to that voice as if God spoke directly to us—then we are never going to be able to clearly hear the voice of God for ourselves.

When you begin to recognize the voice of God, He will take you from where you are to where you need to be!

Knowing and recognizing God's voice comes by spending time in His presence. As you pray, read and meditate on God's Word and begin to develop a relationship with Him, you will begin to recognize His prompting and leading in your life.

When you know His voice, you will know His purpose. You will then be led into His perfect will, and your every need will be provided.

People are yearning to know the voice of God. If you are willing to stand up and get into His presence and discover His direction—not born of sensory mechanisms, but born in the spirit of prayer—nothing will be able to stop the outpouring of His glory in these last days!

COVENANT BLESSINGS
FOR GOD'S GUIDANCE

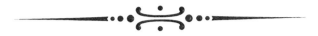

UNDERSTANDING

And of the children of Issachar, which were men that had understanding of the times, to know what Israel ought to do; the heads of them were two hundred; and all their brethren were at their commandment (1 Chronicles 12:32).

But there is a spirit in man: and the inspiration of the Almighty giveth them understanding (Job 32:8).

Folly is joy to him that is destitute of wisdom: but a man of understanding walketh uprightly (Proverb 15:21).

And we know that the Son of God is come, and hath given us an understanding, that we may know him that is true, and we are in him that is true, even in his Son Jesus Christ. This is the true God, and eternal life (1 John 5:20).

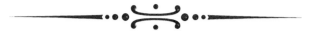

Faith comes by hearing and understanding, and is produced by the Word of God. Understanding brings knowledge, and knowledge brings trust, and trust is faith! If I trust you, I have faith in you.

Understanding is produced by the Word of God. What you understand you can have faith in. It's the simplest, yet most powerful analogy in the world.

The Bible says, "Lean not unto thine own understanding. In all thy ways acknowledge Him" (Proverbs 3:5b,6).

How do you acknowledge Him? You draw attention to Him, and you magnify Him. As you do so, your understanding becomes vivid and you receive clear direction!

It is the breath of Almighty God that gives you understanding. Do you desire understanding? All you have to do is ask for it, and He will give you everything you will need to know to propel you through every situation!

COVENANT BLESSINGS
FOR GOD'S GUIDANCE

VISION

Where there is no vision, the people perish: but he that keepeth the law, happy is he (Proverb 29:18).

I will stand upon my watch, and set me upon the tower, and will watch to see what he will say unto me, and what I shall answer when I am reproved.

And the Lord answered me, and said, Write the vision, and make it plain upon tables, that he may run that readeth it. For the vision is yet for an appointed time, but at the end it shall speak, and not lie: though it tarry, wait for it; because it will surely come, it will not tarry (Habakkuk 2:1-3).

Cast not away therefore your confidence, which hath great recompence of reward. For ye have need of patience, that, after ye have done the will of God, ye might receive the promise.

For yet a little while, and he that shall come will come, and will not tarry (Hebrews 10:35-37).

INSPIRING INSIGHTS
by Rod Parsley

What would you attempt for God if you knew it was impossible to fail? Well, what is stopping you?

Once you grasp God's vision for your life you will no longer be satisfied with church as usual. You won't be satisfied with a six-foot icicle standing behind the pulpit spouting his three points and a poem. You will cry, "Where are the signs and wonders? Where are the miracles? Where are the revelation and the demonstration?"

Vision is foreknowledge from a thought derived from the spirit or heart and not from the sensory information. Where there is no vision, or prophetic voice, people cast off restraint and run wild.

God desires us to operate in His vision for our lives. Vision sets boundaries of protection and provision. When we operate in His vision, we have the assurance of knowing that He will take care of and provide for our every need!

COVENANT BLESSINGS
FOR GOD'S GUIDANCE

WISDOM

The fear of the Lord is the beginning of wisdom: a good understanding have all they that do his commandments: his praise endureth for ever (Psalm 111:10).

He layeth up sound wisdom for the righteous: he is a buckler to them that walk uprightly (Proverb 2:6,7).

And wisdom and knowledge shall be the stability of thy times, and strength of salvation: the fear of the Lord is his treasure (Isaiah 33:6).

Daniel answered and said, Blessed be the name of God for ever and ever: for wisdom and might are his: And he changeth the times and the seasons: he removeth kings, and setteth up kings: he giveth wisdom unto the wise, and knowledge to them that know understanding (Daniel 2:20,21).

When you made the decision to call Jesus your Lord, you transferred the dictatorship of your life from your mental capacities to His spiritual wealth. You moved from your inability and lack of wisdom to His ability and His wisdom to direct the affairs of your life tomorrow.

And may I point out: God is as acquainted with your tomorrow as you are with your yesterday. God knows your future!

The writer of the book of Proverbs, the wisest man who ever lived, was given anything he wanted by God. When asked what he desired, Solomon responded, "I want wisdom."

What is wisdom? It is the ability to use knowledge! You also can have wisdom—all you need to do is ask!

The Bible says wsdom is the principle thing. Love her and she shall love you. Exalt her and she shall exalt you. (Proverb 4:7.) How do you get wisdom? You get it by serving God's people.

ROD PARSLEY CELEBRATING

REPAIRING THE BREACH • RAISING THE STANDARD

• REAPING THE HARVEST •

20th ANNIVERSARY

COVENANT BLESSINGS
for
Your Christian
Walk

COVENANT BLESSINGS
FOR YOUR CHRISTIAN WALK

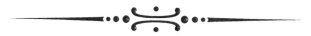

ENCOURAGEMENT

And David was greatly distressed; for the people spake of stoning him, because the soul of all the people was grieved, every man for his sons and for his daughters: but David encouraged himself in the Lord his God (1 Samuel 30:6).

Be of good courage, and he shall strengthen your heart, all ye that hope in the Lord (Psalm 31:24).

Why art thou cast down, O my soul? and why art thou disquieted within me? hope in God: for I shall yet praise him, who is the health of my countenance, and my God (Psalm 43:5).

Let my heart be sound in thy statutes; that I be not ashamed. My soul fainteth for thy salvation: but I hope in thy word (Psalm 119:80,81).

Happy is he that hath the God of Jacob for his help, whose hope is in the Lord his God (Psalm 146:5).

You have words of encouragement that no one else has. You need to offer encouraging words, because you may speak life into someone's situation that otherwise would not have been there.

If you are searching, Jesus has the provision. If you need help, He has the power to deliver you. If you need encouragement, He has the words you need to hear.

Each one of us goes through times when no one knows that we go home at night and put our heads on our pillows and weep tears of discouragement.

It is during these moments that it seems no one or nothing can relieve the pain and the fear. It seems as though we are walking through hell. We are encouraging everyone else, but no one is encouraging us.

There we are at the bottom, but all of a sudden we hear a sweet small voice say, "Everything is going to be all right. Be encouraged! Joy is about to eclipse your life like the noonday sun!"

COVENANT BLESSINGS
FOR YOUR CHRISTIAN WALK

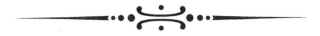

ENDURANCE

And ye shall be hated of all men for my name's sake: but he that endureth to the end shall be saved (Matthew 10:22).

Thou therefore endure hardness, as a good soldier of Jesus Christ (2 Timothy 2:3).

But call to remembrance the former days, in which, after ye were illuminated, ye endured a great fight of afflictions; Cast not away therefore your confidence, which hath great recompence of reward (Hebrews 10:32,35).

Wherefore seeing we also are compassed about with so great a cloud of witnesses, let us lay aside every weight, and the sin which doth so easily beset us, and let us run with patience the race that is set before us, Looking unto Jesus the author and finisher of our faith; who for the joy that was set before him endured the cross, despising the shame, and is set down at the right hand of the throne of God (Hebrews 12:1,2).

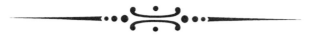

Sentenced to prison as a conscientious objector to the war, Howard Carter brought the revelation of the nine gifts of the Holy Spirit to us. Tormented with tuberculosis at 17, his death certificate signed while he was still breathing, the great apostle, missionary and statesman, Dr. Lester Sumrall brought the revelation of spirit, soul and body to us. Inspired by the words impossible, incurable and insurmountable—these are they who are not called great because they never failed but because they refused to quit.

The race is not to the swift but to those who rise fearless in the face of defeat. Though tempted by compromise and complacency, they are resolute in their assault against the demon of surrender.

There will be 1,000 at your left hand and 10,000 at your right hand who will surrender to distraction, submit to defeat and succumb to the daily onslaught of the devil. They will become casualties of the crippling condition of compromise.

The prize is reserved not for those who begin but for those who finish the race, those who will not be denied their position, delayed in their pursuit or detoured on the path to their promise.

COVENANT BLESSINGS
FOR YOUR CHRISTIAN WALK

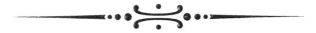

EXPECTANCY

The wicked shall be turned into hell, and all the nations that forget God. For the needy shall not alway be forgotten: the expectation of the poor shall not perish for ever (Psalm 9:17,18).

Let not thine heart envy sinners: but be thou in the fear of the Lord all the day long. For surely there is an end; and thine expectation shall not be cut off (Proverb 23:17,18).

So shall the knowledge of wisdom be unto thy soul: when thou hast found it, then there shall be a reward, and thy expectation shall not be cut off (Proverb 24:14).

According to my earnest expectation and my hope, that in nothing I shall be ashamed, but that with all boldness, as always, so now also Christ shall be magnified in my body, whether it be by life, or by death. For to me to live is Christ, and to die is gain (Philippians 1:20,21).

INSPIRING INSIGHTS
by Rod Parsley

The atmosphere of expectancy is the breeding ground of miracles.

Father, in the name of Jesus, anoint us to live with expectancy. Allow us to look for a miracle with every glance of our eyes.

If you can get a level of expectancy about what God is going to do in your life, even before your feet hit the floor, you will literally shake the foundations of hell. Nothing you can set your mind to will be impossible!

The pain of your past will give way to the expectancy of the miracle that just may be in your next step, next prayer, next shout, or the next song. Your answer is on the way!

❖❖❖

Your level of expectancy increases when you realize God is present to give you whatever you will ask!

COVENANT BLESSINGS
FOR YOUR CHRISTIAN WALK

FAITH

But they have not all obeyed the gospel. For Esaias saith, Lord, who hath believed our report? So then faith cometh by hearing, and hearing by the word of God (Romans 10:16,17).

Fight the good fight of faith, lay hold on eternal life, whereunto thou art also called, and hast professed a good profession before many witnesses (1 Timothy 6:12).

Now faith is the substance of things hoped for, the evidence of things not seen (Hebrews 11:1).

That the trial of your faith, being much more precious than of gold that perisheth, though it be tried with fire, might be found unto praise and honour and glory at the appearing of Jesus Christ (1 Peter 1:7).

For whatsoever is born of God overcometh the world: and this is the victory that overcometh the world, even our faith (1 John 5:4).

Right now you can make a decision! You can allow your mountain to move your faith, or you can allow your faith to move your mountain.

If you are going to survive the perils of perilous times you need to have a faith that knows. You need to have a faith that grows. You need to have a faith rooted and grounded in the Word of God.

Perfect faith can only exist where the will of God is known.

Faith is not some mystical substance that is whirled around in cauldrons in the realm of the spirit and dumped out by angels. Faith is just good, old-fashioned, hard-working knowledge.

Faith says, I shall have it. You shall have whatever it is you are believing God for—healing, deliverance, financial breakthrough or the salvation of a lost loved one. You shall have it!

COVENANT BLESSINGS
FOR YOUR CHRISTIAN WALK

HOPE

Hope deferred maketh the heart sick: but when the desire cometh, it is a tree of life (Proverb 13:12).

For we are saved by hope: but hope that is seen is not hope: for what a man seeth, why doth he yet hope for (Romans 8:24)?

If in this life only we have hope in Christ, we are of all men most miserable. But now is Christ risen from the dead, and become the firstfruits of them that slept (1 Corinthians 15:19,20).

Wherein God, willing more abundantly to shew unto the heirs of promise the immutability of his counsel, confirmed it by an oath: that by two immutable things, in which it was impossible for God to lie, we might have a strong consolation, who have fled for refuge to lay hold upon the hope set before us: Which hope we have as an anchor of the soul, both sure and stedfast, and which entereth into that within the veil (Hebrews 6:17-19).

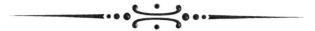

We have hope beyond the scope of human limitations.

The apex of our hope in God—the crown jewel of our faith is this: Jesus is not here. He is risen as He said—He pried the keys of death, hell and the grave out of the unyielding hands of the Antichrist. He locked up skepticism and fear, and today we have hope!

If you have faith and love without hope, then you have despair! When trouble comes without hope as a foundation, you will give up and quit.

Faith in God can give you hope when you're facing the fiery furnace that has been heated seven times hotter than it should be. You can be assured God is going to command the crackling flames not to kindle upon you.

He will also cause you to pass through the flood without it drowning you. Faith in God can turn your midnight into dawn and your jail cell into a prayer meeting!

COVENANT BLESSINGS
FOR YOUR CHRISTIAN WALK

Knowing God

And such as do wickedly against the covenant shall he corrupt by flatteries: but the people that do know their God shall be strong, and do exploits (Daniel 11:32).

Yea doubtless, and I count all things but loss for the excellency of the knowledge of Christ Jesus my Lord: for whom I have suffered the loss of all things, and do count them but dung, that I may win Christ, and be found in him, not having mine own righteousness, which is of the law, but that which is through the faith of Christ, the righteousness which is of God by faith: that I may know him, and the power of his resurrection, and the fellowship of his sufferings, being made conformable unto his death; if by any means I might attain unto the resurrection of the dead.

Not as though I had already attained, either were already perfect: but I follow after, if that I may apprehend that for which also I am apprehended of Christ Jesus (Philippians 3:8-12).

INSPIRING INSIGHTS
by Rod Parsley

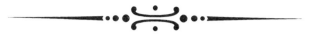

Every fresh, new golden era of human history has been preceded by the devotion and righteous passion of one or more individuals who knew their God and knew where they were going.

The church has become professional in doing the work of the Lord, but it has forgotten the Lord of the work! What God wants from us is not religion, but relationship.

In the midst of the trials of life, it is one thing to know God. It is another thing to have God say, "I know this man, I know his heart and I know he will faithfully serve me." I want to be that man.

Daniel was a man who prayed three times a day—not once a week. Daniel spent time with God, so when trials came, he knew Him. He knew He would deliver him . . . but really, if He didn't, Daniel knew it would be alright anyway, because he had a relationship with God built on prayer.

COVENANT BLESSINGS
FOR YOUR CHRISTIAN WALK

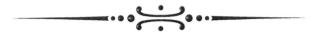

OBEDIENCE

And Samuel said, Hath the Lord as great delight in burnt offerings and sacrifices, as in obeying the voice of the Lord? Behold, to obey is better than sacrifice, and to hearken than the fat of rams (1 Samuel 15:22)

Come now, and let us reason together, saith the Lord: though your sins be as scarlet, they shall be as white as snow; though they be red like crimson, they shall be as wool. If ye be willing and obedient, ye shall eat the good of the land (Isaiah 1:18,19).

But this thing commanded I them, saying, Obey my voice, and I will be your God, and ye shall be my people: and walk ye in all the ways that I have commanded you, that it may be well unto you (Jeremiah 7:23).

And being made perfect, he [Jesus] became the author of eternal salvation unto all them that obey him (Hebrews 5:9).

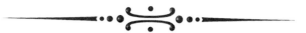

When you are obedient and faithful, you will be so prosperous you will have money to lend to others who are less fortunate than you. You won't need a master credit card—you just need the Master!

God is looking for obedience. He is looking for people who will hear the word spoken prophetically, lay hold on it, make it their own and respond to it as if God, Himself had spoken it directly to them.

Obedience brings the perpetual supply of God into your life.

The only cure to keep the body of Christ going forward is obedience, because disobedience is lost time. God cannot bless you past your last act of disobedience. You have to go back and do what He originally spoke for you to do, so you can unlock His provision once again!

Obedience is the hinge on the door that swings open into the blessing of God for your life.

COVENANT BLESSINGS
FOR YOUR CHRISTIAN WALK

POWER

But ye shall receive power, after that the Holy Ghost is come upon you: and ye shall be witnesses unto me both in Jerusalem, and in all Judaea, and in Samaria, and unto the uttermost part of the earth (Acts 1:8).

For I am not ashamed of the gospel of Christ: for it is the power of God unto salvation to every one that believeth; to the Jew first, and also to the Greek (Romans 1:16).

For our gospel came not unto you in word only, but also in power, and in the Holy Ghost, and in much assurance; as ye know what manner of men we were among you for your sake (1 Thessalonians 1:5).

For the preaching of the cross is to them that perish foolishness; but unto us which are saved it is the power of God (1 Corinthians 1:18).

The process of life is the process of exchange. God cannot pour more into us until we give something out.

Though Pentecost meant power to the disciples, may I remind you, it also meant prison for them. Though it meant endowment with power, it also meant banishment from organized religion! It is time to count the cost!

Power is the divine prerogative of God to operate in your life.

God wants to give you power—power over depravity; power over sin; power over temptation. He wants to give you power over every plot and satanic scheme against you!

You have power over the very thing that is troubling your life. You have power over all the power of the enemy!

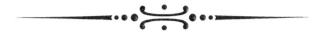
REPENTANCE

From that time Jesus began to preach, and to say, Repent: for the kingdom of heaven is at hand (Matthew 4:17).

Or despisest thou the riches of his goodness and forbearance and longsuffering; not knowing that the goodness of God leadeth thee to repentance (Romans 2:4)?

Now I rejoice, not that ye were made sorry, but that ye sorrowed to repentance: for ye were made sorry after a godly manner, that ye might receive damage by us in nothing. For godly sorrow worketh repentance to salvation not to be repented of: but the sorrow of the world worketh death (2 Corinthians 7:9,10).

The Lord is not slack concerning his promise, as some men count slackness; but is longsuffering to us-ward, not willing that any should perish, but that all should come to repentance (2 Peter 3:9).

Repentance is not a bad thing, it is a good thing. "It is the goodness of God that leads us to repentance." If you will allow Him to touch your sin-stained heart, He will bring you to your knees once again.

Without conviction there can be no change, and we not only need a change of mind, we need a change of heart—a heart turned toward God.

The very first words of Jesus in Matthew 4:17 are, "Repent for the kingdom of heaven is at hand." Jesus will say nothing else until this is done.

Why? Because the heart of the human problem is the problem of the human heart. It is time to return to the discarded values of the past and to call people back to repentance.

Repentance means to change your mind about God and toward God. We must repent of the sins of commission—doing what we know not to do. We must also repent of the sins of omission—not doing what we know we should.

COVENANT BLESSINGS
FOR YOUR CHRISTIAN WALK

SOVEREIGNTY

Thy kingdom is an everlasting kingdom, and thy dominion endureth throughout all generations. The Lord upholdeth all that fall, and raiseth up all those that be bowed down (Psalm 145:13,14).

And I will make her that halted a remnant, and her that was cast far off a strong nation: and the Lord shall reign over them in mount Zion from henceforth, even for ever (Micah 4:7).

Now unto him that is able to keep you from falling, and to present you faultless before the presence of his glory with exceeding joy, to the only wise God our Saviour, be glory and majesty, dominion and power, both now and ever. Amen (Jude 24,25).

And the seventh angel sounded; and there were great voices in heaven, saying, the kingdoms of this world are become the kingdoms of our Lord, and of his Christ; and he shall reign for ever and ever (Revelation 11:15).

INSPIRING INSIGHTS
by Rod Parsley

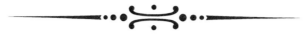

This is my deep definition of sovereignty—He is God, and we are not!

God's kingdom is a theocracy, not a democracy. It's not up for a vote. Christ is our King, and we are His loyal subjects.

God is not an added social event to your calendar once a week; He is God. He is not a spare tire to get you out of your problems; He is God. It is time we pledge our fidelity to Him and allow His sovereign reign in our life.

Jesus Christ stands waiting, ready to pick you up in your broken, useless condition, put you back on the Potter's wheel and begin to mold you into what He wants you to be. But how do you submit to a sovereign God? You submit unto death and you say, "I am willing to die to my will, my way, my hopes, my dreams, my plans and my schemes. I'm placing my whole life in your hands. I am bowing my knee, my heart, my head and my hands in your presence. I am submitting to the sovereignty of God simply because I know You love me."

COVENANT BLESSINGS
FOR YOUR CHRISTIAN WALK

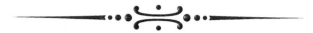

STRENGTH

For thou hast girded me with strength to battle: them that rose up against me hast thou subdued under me (2 Samuel 22:40).

Be of good courage, and he shall strengthen your heart, all ye that hope in the Lord (Psalm 31:24).

The way of the Lord is strength to the upright: but destruction shall be to the workers of iniquity (Proverb 10:29).

The Lord God is my strength, and he will make my feet like hinds' feet, and he will make me to walk upon mine high places. To the chief singer on my stringed instruments (Habakkuk 3:19).

And he said unto me, My grace is sufficient for thee: for my strength is made perfect in weakness. Most gladly therefore will I rather glory in my infirmities, that the power of Christ may rest upon me (2 Corinthians 12:9).

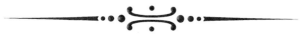

We get our strength on the front lines of conflict. That is where the anointing is.

The purpose of God in your life is to end weakness. Everything He does, all His purposes are to bring strength to your life. Only by struggle can strength be had.

God has a greater opinion of who He is in you than you do. He believes you're going to win. He believes you are going to make it to the top. He believes you have strength inside of you to destroy every diabolical scheme of the darkened regions of the demonic underworld. God has confidence in your victory!

The Lord has provided a position of strength, power and authority in His kingdom for those who operate within the boundaries of their position in His kingdom.

❖❖❖

God will be your strength when you don't have the power to pray or even lift your head from your pillow!

TRUST

The God of my rock; in him will I trust: he is my shield, and the horn of my salvation, my high tower, and my refuge, my saviour; thou savest me from violence (2 Samuel 22:3).

Some trust in chariots, and some in horses: but we will remember the name of the Lord our God (Proverb 20:7).

He that is of a proud heart stirreth up strife: but he that putteth his trust in the Lord shall be made fat (Proverb 28:25).

Behold, God is my salvation; I will trust, and not be afraid: for the Lord Jehovah is my strength and my song; he also is become my salvation (Isaiah 12:2).

And again, I will put my trust in him. And again, behold I and the children which God hath given me (Hebrews 2:13).

God will never create a life for you which will make Him unnecessary. As you trust Him, He will be your hope and strength for every situation!

God will deliver you out of all your fears if you will just trust Him.

What is faith? It is steadfast confidence, assurance and trust. The bottom line of faith is trust. Do you trust Him?

To trust Jesus means to take Him at His Word.

God is not asking you to blindly trust Him. He does not demand faith until He has proven himself faithful! The fact of the matter is, if you can learn to trust Him, you can find the secret place.

The secret place is the place you find in God where the evil one cannot touch you (1 John 5:18)!

COVENANT
BLESSINGS
of
God's Promises

COVENANT BLESSINGS
OF GOD'S PROMISE

ACCEPTANCE

Then Peter opened his mouth, and said, Of a truth I perceive that God is no respecter of persons: but in every nation he that feareth him, and worketh righteousness, is accepted with him (Acts 10:34,35).

We are confident, I say, and willing rather to be absent from the body, and to be present with the Lord. Wherefore we labour, that, whether present or absent, we may be accepted of him (2 Corinthians 5:8,9).

Blessed be the God and Father of our Lord Jesus Christ, who hath blessed us with all spiritual blessings in heavenly places in Christ: According as he hath chosen us in him before the foundation of the world, that we should be holy and without blame before him in love:
Having predestinated us unto the adoption of children by Jesus Christ to himself, according to the good pleasure of his will, to the praise of the glory of his grace, wherein he hath made us accepted in the beloved (Ephesians 1:3-6).

$\mathbf{Y}$ou are accepted in the household of faith. It doesn't matter where you came from or what your credentials are. When you proclaimed Jesus as Lord, you were accepted in the beloved. God immediately transferred you out of the kingdom of darkness and into the Kingdom of His dear Son.

$\mathbf{A}$ny gospel that tells you that you are anything other than accepted in the beloved is a lie from the smoky black pit of hell. Jesus did not die on Calvary for you to become a doormat for the devil. He died to bring you into His blessing.

$\mathbf{Y}$ou were accepted in the beloved when you pronounced Jesus as your Lord and Savior. All you need is divine endorsement, which comes from being in God's will. When you have the Father's endorsement all of heaven backs you.

$\mathbf{A}$cceptance is the product of grace to allow you to come boldly before the throne of God and find grace to help in time of need. You, who were sometimes far off, have been made nigh by the blood of Christ. No other sacrifice is needed, because you have been accepted.

COVENANT BLESSINGS
OF GOD'S PROMISE

ANGELS

This poor man cried, and the Lord heard him, and saved him out of all his troubles. The angel of the Lord encampeth round about them that fear him, and delivereth them (Psalm 34:6,7).

For he shall give his angels charge over thee, to keep thee in all thy ways. They shall bear thee up in their hands, lest thou dash thy foot against a stone. Thou shalt tread upon the lion and adder: the young lion and the dragon shalt thou trample under feet (Psalm 91:11-13).

Bless the Lord, ye his angels, that excel in strength, that do his commandments, hearkening unto the voice of his word (Psalm 103:20).

But to which of the angels said he at any time, Sit on my right hand, until I make thine enemies thy footstool? Are they not all ministering spirits, sent forth to minister for them who shall be heirs of salvation (Hebrews 1:13,14).

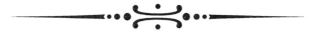

We have the authority to send forth ministering spirits, or angels, into the fields to reap our harvest.

When you pray, God dispatches angels to begin carrying out and bringing that answer toward you. However they must come from the third heaven, where they are, down to the earth realm. (Daniel 10:12,13.) In order to get into the earth realm, they have to go through that area of Satan's domain. They are warring against the demonic spirits on your behalf in order to bring your answer to pass!

Your angels are fighting to bring you your answer. Don't cast away your confidence if you don't see the answer right away. Remember, God heard your prayer the moment you prayed, and it was sealed in heaven. It will be answered and manifested in the natural realm.

God will intervene in your life through angelic activity as you prophesy His Word over your situation. Angels stand positioned ready to bring your answer to pass.

COVENANT BLESSINGS
OF GOD'S PROMISE

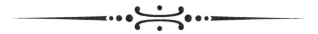

ASSURANCE

And the work of righteousness shall be peace; and the effect of righteousness quietness and assurance for ever (Isaiah 32:17).

Therefore if any man be in Christ, he is a new creature: old things are passed away; behold, all things are become new (2 Corinthians 5:17).

That their hearts might be comforted, being knit together in love, and unto all riches of the full assurance of understanding, to the acknowledgment of the mystery of God, and of the Father, and of Christ (Colossians 2:2).

Let us draw near with a true heart in full assurance of faith, having our hearts sprinkled from an evil conscience, and our bodies washed with pure water.
Let us hold fast the profession of our faith without wavering; (for he is faithful that promised, (Hebrews 10:22,23).

Jesus has promised if you call on Him, He will answer. Before you can speak His name, He will be found with you. (Jeremiah 29:13,14.) That means if you ask, you are forgiven. It means if you want assurance, you have it. If you want victory, then it is yours!

You have a blessed assurance to know you have a strong tower you can run to in times of need. (Proverb 18:10.)

Though hell comes and tempests rage, you have on the inside of you a deep-seated assurance. Like the wings of the morning, you are going to wing your way to the snow capped mountain peaks of the pavilions of God's glory. You are going to find yourself stationed in a place called heaven, where the streets are not paved with gold, they are made out of it.

It is a place where the river of life proceeds from the throne of God. There you will suffer no more, cry no more, die no more and say goodbye no more. You have the assurance of where you are going, because you have Jesus living on the inside of you!

COVENANT BLESSINGS
OF GOD'S PROMISE

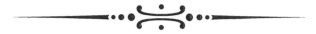

CONFIDENCE

And to make all men see what is the fellowship of the mystery, which from the beginning of the world hath been hid in God, who created all things by Jesus Christ: to the intent that now unto the principalities and powers in heavenly places might be known by the church the manifold wisdom of God, according to the eternal purpose which he purposed in Christ Jesus our Lord: in whom we have boldness and access with confidence by the faith of him (Ephesians 3:9-12).

I thank my God upon every remembrance of you, always in every prayer of mine for you all making request with joy, for your fellowship in the gospel from the first day until now; being confident of this very thing, that he which hath begun a good work in you will perform it until the day of Jesus Christ (Philippians 1:3-6).

Cast not away therefore your confidence, which hath great recompence of reward. For ye have need of patience, that, after ye have done the will of God, ye might receive the promise (Hebrews 10:35,36).

INSPIRING INSIGHTS
by Rod Parsley

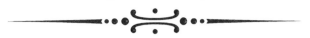

God wants you to have enough confidence in Him that, regardless of what you are going through, you always remember you are going through. You are coming out on the other side!

God has more confidence in you than you have in you! He has confidence you are going to possess the land, overcome the giants and take what's in their hand!

The Lord wants you to have steadfast confidence, trust and assurance that He is who He says He is . . . He can do what He says He can do and He has what He says He has. If you believe that, then you have confidence. Confidence, however, does not lead you away from the conflict. It is a character builder, and character is built in the arena of your conflict! It's only when you're in the battle that you find out of what you are really made!

God has confidence that you will take His Word, appropriate it in your life and begin to act upon it. Thereby, He can release His kingdom into this earth and produce the greatest harvest and revival the world has ever known!

20th ANNIVERSARY

COVENANT BLESSINGS
OF GOD'S PROMISE

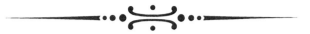

CONTENTMENT

Not that I speak in respect of want: for I have learned, in whatsoever state I am, therewith to be content. I know both how to be abased, and I know how to abound: every where and in all things I am instructed both to be full and to be hungry, both to abound and to suffer need. I can do all things through Christ which strengtheneth me (Philippians 4:11-13).

But godliness with contentment is great gain. For we brought nothing into this world, and it is certain we can carry nothing out. And having food and raiment let us be therewith content (1 Timothy 6:6-8).

Let your conversation be without covetousness; and be content with such things as ye have: for he hath said, I will never leave thee, nor forsake thee. So that we may boldly say, The Lord is my helper, and I will not fear what man shall do unto me (Hebrews 13:5,6).

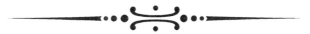

The body of Christ is going to come to the point of maturity when we can take one step and immediately be in the presence of God. We will immediately begin hearing His voice, but we will be content if He does not speak.

Paul said, "I know how to be content." Contentment means to be settled, stilled, silenced, reverent or receptive. It is not to be quiet in order to get God to say something to you but, rather, just being quiet to let Him commune with you.

You must learn how to be content with where you are and knowing you are in the will of God. Your steps are ordered of the Lord, and He will take you where you need to be. (Psalm 37:23.)

God will never allow you to be content with where you are in Him. However, the Bible says He is changing us from glory to glory by Christ Jesus. (2 Corinthians 3:18.) Therefore, your greatest satisfaction should be your dissatisfaction with where you are in God and what you're accomplishing for Him!

COVENANT BLESSINGS
OF GOD'S PROMISE

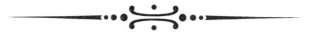

DELIVERANCE

Thou art my hiding place; thou shalt preserve me from trouble; thou shalt compass me about with songs of deliverance. Selah (Psalm 32:7).

Many are the afflictions of the righteous: but the Lord delivereth him out of them all (Psalm 34:19).

Shadrach, Meshach, and Abednego, answered and said to the king, O Nebuchadnezzar, we are not careful to answer thee in this matter. Our God whom we serve is able to deliver us from the burning fiery furnace, and he will deliver us out of thine hand, O king (Daniel 3:16,17).

But we had the sentence of death in ourselves, that we should not trust in ourselves, but in God which raiseth the dead: who delivered us from so great a death, and doth deliver: in whom we trust that he will yet deliver us (2 Corinthians 1:9,10).

When God delivers you from something, He always delivers you to something else, and it is always something better.

The first step to freedom is confession. In order to stay free, fill your spirit with the Word.

Freedom is never granted voluntarily by the oppressor, it must be demanded by the oppressed. When the enemy tries to invade your life, like a flood Jesus will raise up a standard against him. (Isaiah 59:19.) The Lord wants you to demand your independence of Satan's occupation!

A breakthrough is a sudden burst of the advance knowledge of God which will propel us through every line of Satan's defense.

Men who know they have been delivered are men who can never be bound again.

Haven't you come to the end of Loneliness Boulevard and Wits-end Corner? It is not your effort that is going to produce your freedom. It is God's effort on your behalf!

COVENANT BLESSINGS
OF GOD'S PROMISE

FAVOR

And the Lord gave the people favour in the sight of the Egyptians, so that they lent unto them such things as they required. And they spoiled the Egyptians (Exodus 12:36).

But let all those that put their trust in thee rejoice: let them ever shout for joy, because thou defendest them: let them also that love thy name be joyful in thee. For thou, Lord, wilt bless the righteous; with favour wilt thou compass him as with a shield (Psalm 5:11,12).

Blessed is the man that heareth me, watching daily at my gates, waiting at the posts of my doors. For whoso findeth me findeth life, and shall obtain favour of the Lord (Proverb 8:34,35).

A good man obtaineth favour of the Lord: but a man of wicked devices will he condemn (Proverb 12:2).

You can't earn the favor of God, you can't buy it and you can't find it. Rather, He anoints you with it. You have supernatural favor!

Like the Israelites who came out of Egyptian bondage, the Lord is going to bless you with favor. People who don't like you are going to bless you. People who don't like to be around you are going to lay down their coats for you to walk on so you won't step in the mud.

People who have made fun of you, because of your stand for healing, are going to call you when they are sick. Favor is coming to you!

The more time you give to God, the more effective you will be. You will receive multiple blessings. God's multiple blessings are His favor.

When you take your eyes off of your circumstances and put your eyes on God, soon He will give you the ability, the favor, the power and the authority to do more than you could ever imagine you could do!

COVENANT BLESSINGS
OF GOD'S PROMISE

HEALING

He sent his word, and healed them, and delivered them from their destructions (Psalm 107:20).

But he was wounded for our transgressions, he was bruised for our iniquities: the chastisement of our peace was upon him; and with his stripes we are healed (Isaiah 53:5).

Because Christ also suffered for us, leaving us an example, that ye should follow his steps: who did no sin, neither was guile found in his mouth: who his own self bare our sins in his own body on the tree, that we, being dead to sins, should live unto righteousness: by whose stripes ye were healed (1 Peter 2:21,24).

Is any sick among you? let him call for the elders of the church; and let them pray over him, anointing him with oil in the name of the Lord: and the prayer of faith shall save the sick, and the Lord shall raise him up; and if he have committed sins, they shall be forgiven him (James 5:14,15).

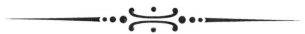

There are still those who ask, "Is God even *able* to heal?" *Able?* He set the world spinning upside down and commanded the oceans not to spill a drop. When your body isn't functioning correctly, who better is there to turn to than the One who created you?

Get a word from God—and *stick with it.* Even if you have to paper your walls with little yellow "stick'em" notes, keep His words of faith and healing always before you.

❖❖❖

It doesn't matter if the doctor looks at you and says you have to die and cannot live. Begin to seek God for the anointing. Your darkest hour will soon be like the glistening radiance of the noonday sun.

The three most asked questions regarding healing are: "Will God heal me?" "Can God heal me?" and "Is it God's will for me to be healed?"

The Bible still declares, "Today is the day of salvation and now is the appointed time." (2 Corinthians 6:2.) Salvation means healing, deliverance, prosperity—whatever you need!

COVENANT BLESSINGS
OF GOD'S PROMISE

MIND

And be not conformed to this world: but be ye transformed by the renewing of your mind, that ye may prove what is that good, and acceptable, and perfect, will of God (Romans 12:2).

(For the weapons of our warfare are not carnal, but mighty through God to the pulling down of strong holds;) Casting down imaginations, and every high thing that exalteth itself against the knowledge of God, and bringing into captivity every thought to the obedience of Christ (2 Corinthians 10:4,5).

And be renewed in the spirit of your mind; and that ye put on the new man, which after God is created in righteousness and true holiness (Ephesians 4:23,24).

Wherefore gird up the loins of your mind, be sober, and hope to the end for the grace that is to be brought unto you at the revelation of Jesus Christ (1 Peter 1:13).

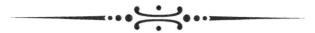

The best mind cannot compete with a blessed mind!

One of the greatest areas, as the body of Christ, we need to change is our minds from a missionary barrel mentality to a prosperity mentality. A poverty ridden mind is not God's plan for you. You need to change your mind!

In order to have the blessing of God, you need a mind that is renewed to His Word. You need a will that is submitted to the purposes and plans of God but not broken. You need emotions that are in control and that do not control you. You need to learn to live a fasted lifestyle.

Your mind must be changed concerning your finances. You are not a child of lack, you are a child of abundance. You are not a child of less, you are a child of more. You are not a child of poverty, you are a child of provision!

God does not want you to be double-minded. Listen to your spirit and to the Bible concerning His plan for your life, and you will not be confused!

COVENANT BLESSINGS
OF GOD'S PROMISE

PROTECTION

He that dwelleth in the secret place of the most High shall abide under the shadow of the Almighty. I will say of the Lord, He is my refuge and my fortress: my God; in him will I trust. Surely he shall deliver thee from the snare of the fowler, and from the noisome pestilence. He shall cover thee with his feathers, and under his wings shalt thou trust: his truth shall be thy shield and buckler (Psalm 91:1-4).

In the fear of the Lord is strong confidence: and his children shall have a place of refuge. The fear of the Lord is a fountain of life, to depart from the snares of death (Proverb 14:26,27).

O Lord, thou art my God; I will exalt thee, I will praise thy name; for thou hast done wonderful things; thy counsels of old are faithfulness and truth. For thou hast been a strength to the poor, a strength to the needy in his distress, a refuge from the storm, a shadow from the heat, when the blast of the terrible ones is as a storm against the wall (Isaiah 25:1,4).

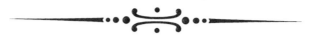

A young man, holding onto a rope, was dangling hundreds of feet above the ground from a hot air balloon. In amazement and horror, a crowd began to gather around as they saw him holding on for his life.

When the balloon finally landed safely, one person asked, "How did you hold on?" He responded, "I didn't hold on. I took the rope and wrapped it around myself and let it hold onto me."

In your darkest hour of adversity Jesus will be your life line, and He will cling to you and bring you safely into a place of refuge!

❖❖❖

When at times it seems as though refuge forsakes me, sometimes I just pretend to reach over and take the hand of Jesus.

You can do the same. He walks with you right now, and you can hold His hand.

The devil can't do anything about your tomorrow as long as you are operating in the vision of God. The Lord is a refuge and fortress and has built a hedge of protection around you.

COVENANT BLESSINGS
OF GOD'S PROMISE

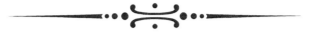

REVIVAL

Wilt thou not revive us again: that thy people may rejoice in thee? Shew us thy mercy, O Lord, and grant us thy salvation (Psalm 85:6,7).

They that dwell under his shadow shall return; they shall revive as the corn, and grow as the vine: the scent thereof shall be as the wine of Lebanon (Hosea 14:7).

O Lord, I have heard thy speech, and was afraid: O Lord, revive thy work in the midst of the years, in the midst of the years make known; in wrath remember mercy (Habakkuk 3:2).

Repent ye therefore, and be converted, that your sins may be blotted out, when the times of refreshing shall come from the presence of the Lord; and he shall send Jesus Christ, which before was preached unto you: whom the heaven must receive until the times of restitution of all things, which God hath spoken by the mouth of all his holy prophets since the world began (Acts 3:19-21).

We are the generation destined for the experiential manifestation and revelation of the glory of God.

The major indicator of revival is repentance and a contrite spirit before God. Revival is not when the world gets right; revival is when the church gets right.

A true culture-shaking revival takes place when the moral climate of our city is changed and its effect is felt throughout the nation. I believe it has begun—not only in America, but also all around the globe.

Revival will begin when we become broken before God and we get a lost world upon our heart. It is our responsibility to use the giftings and callings of God to bring revival to our city, nation and the world.

We need to stop looking for revival and realize revival is here. The floodgates are open, the heavens are open; the blessing of God is being poured out everywhere. It is time to throw your umbrella away and get into the flow of revival.

COVENANT BLESSINGS OF GOD'S PROMISE

VICTORY

O sing unto the Lord a new song; for he hath done marvellous things: his right hand, and his holy arm, hath gotten him the victory. The Lord hath made known his salvation: his righteousness hath he openly shewed in the sight of the heathen. He hath remembered his mercy and his truth toward the house of Israel: all the ends of the earth have seen the salvation of our God (Psalm 98:1-3).

He will swallow up death in victory; and the Lord God will wipe away tears from off all faces; and the rebuke of his people shall he take away from off all the earth: for the Lord hath spoken it (Isaiah 25:8).

And they shall fight against thee; but they shall not prevail against thee; for I am with thee, saith the Lord, to deliver thee (Jeremiah 1:19).

Now thanks be unto God, which always causeth us to triumph in Christ, and maketh manifest the savour of his knowledge by us in every place (2 Corinthians 2:14).

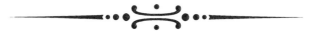

You are destined for battle, which means you are destined for victory!

When you realize your identity in Christ and know His power; then that power will bring you victory. You will have victory over darkness and every demonic force arrayed against you!

When the devil tries to steal your victory announce, "Victory is mine, Devil! I want you to know where I stand. I'm not going backwards. I have my mind set on Jesus. I'm destined for victory. I cannot fail. I receive my victory now!"

Each step you take toward victory means you are on your way to the mountain peak of the blessing of God and trampling devils under your feet every step of the way! There's nothing hell can do to what heaven has blessed!

When you are walking through the trials of life and wonder if you will ever feel the sunlit hills of victory again, know this: everything in your life is a season. Never put a period where God has placed a comma!

ROD PARSLEY CELEBRATING

REPAIRING THE BREACH • RAISING THE STANDARD

REAPING THE HARVEST

20th ANNIVERSARY

COVENANT BLESSINGS
for the
Virtuous
Christian

COVENANT BLESSINGS FOR THE VIRTUOUS CHRISTIAN

COMPASSION

He will turn again, he will have compassion upon us; he will subdue our iniquities; and thou wilt cast all their sins into the depths of the sea (Micah 7:19).

But when he saw the multitudes, he was moved with compassion on them, because they fainted, and were scattered abroad, as sheep having no shepherd (Matthew 9:36).

Finally, be ye all of one mind, having compassion one of another, love as brethren, be pitiful, be courteous: . . . . knowing that ye are thereunto called, that ye should inherit a blessing (1 Peter 3:8,9).

Keep yourselves in the love of God, looking for the mercy of our Lord Jesus Christ unto eternal life. And of some have compassion, making a difference (Jude 21,22).

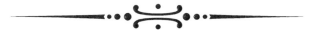

The body of Christ is going to get to the point where sympathy is eclipsed by compassion. The difference is compassion moves you to *do something* about a situation.

It is only when we are moved with compassion that we will look at the multitudes. We will see them hurting, bleeding and dying without Jesus as their Savior or Healer. Compassion is not sorrow; it is an unction to facilitate change.

Compassion produces a divine flow of love from which the anointing issues.

The Bible says, "Jesus was moved with compassion." Translated here, compassion actually means, "His inward parts were wrenched within Him."

When we begin to operate in the same kind of compassion in which Jesus operated, we will then be moved to meet the needs of lost and hurting humanity. We will not tolerate sin and sickness plaguing the lives of people any longer.

COVENANT BLESSINGS FOR THE VIRTUOUS CHRISTIAN

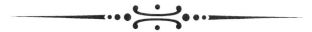

CONVERSATION

Whoso offereth praise glorifieth me: and to him that ordereth his conversation aright will I shew the salvation of God (Psalm 50:23).

A soft answer turneth away wrath: but grievous words stir up anger. The tongue of the wise useth knowledge aright: but the mouth of fools poureth out foolishness (Proverb 15:1,2).

Death and life are in the power of the tongue: and they that love it shall eat the fruit thereof (Proverb 18:21).

Let your speech be alway with grace, seasoned with salt, that ye may know how ye ought to answer every man (Colossians 4:6).

But as he which hath called you is holy, so be ye holy in all manner of conversation; because it is written, Be ye holy; for I am holy (1 Peter 1:15,16).

We abort our own spiritual miracles by the words we utter out of our mouths. We speak words that hurt, words that injure and words that bring death simply because we don't think!

It is imperative that we do not stagger in our conversations. The devil wants to use our words against us so we will say the wrong thing.

❖❖❖

If you want to change the destiny of your life, begin to speak forth the Word of God. His Word needs to be hidden in your heart. It has to be part of you. It has to be a spontaneous reflex action.

You can't think about it then run to get Grandma's Bible and hope and pray for a miracle. You have to realize you are a miracle. You are full of the Word of God; you are the ark of the covenant. Wherever you go, your enemies topple before you, because of that Word. Praise the Lord!

❖❖❖

When you control your tongue, you control your destiny!

COVENANT BLESSINGS FOR THE VIRTUOUS CHRISTIAN

FAITHFULNESS

Thy mercy, O Lord, is in the heavens; and thy faithfulness reacheth unto the clouds (Psalm 36:5).

The enemy shall not exact upon him; nor the son of wickedness afflict him. And I will beat down his foes before his face, and plague them that hate him. But my faithfulness and my mercy shall be with him: and in my name shall his horn be exalted. I will set his hand also in the sea, and his right hand in the rivers. He shall cry unto me, Thou art my father, my God, and the rock of my salvation (Psalm 89:22-26).

Faithful is he that calleth you, who also will do it (1 Thessalonians 5:23,24).

Let us hold fast the profession of our faith without wavering; (for he is faithful that promised) (Hebrews 10:23).

Stay faithful to God . . . never quit . . . never allow bitterness or anger to set in your spirit and your life will become a living temple to glorify His holy name.

Faithful means to be full of faith. Surround yourself with men and women who are full of faith. Why? When you consider the end result of their conduct, you will begin to imitate their faith. Then what God entrusts to you, you can freely entrust to others, because you are faithful!

Base your faith on the God of the Word. The Word is only the tool by which He proves His faithfulness to you. He never demands faithfulness until first he has proven Himself faithful.

Your standing in the kingdom of God is not based upon your status in life! It is based upon your service. It is based upon your faithfulness. Are you faithful over the giftings and callings of God on your life?

COVENANT BLESSINGS FOR THE VIRTUOUS CHRISTIAN

GENTLENESS

Thou hast also given me the shield of thy salvation: and thy right hand hath holden me up, and thy gentleness hath made me great (Psalm 18:35).

But the fruit of the Spirit is love, joy, peace, longsuffering, gentleness, goodness, faith, meekness, temperance: against such there is no law (Galatians 5:22,23).

And the servant of the Lord must not strive; but be gentle unto all men, apt to teach, patient, in meekness instructing those that oppose themselves; if God peradventure will give them repentance to the acknowledging of the truth (2 Timothy 2:24,25).

Put them in mind to be subject to principalities and powers, to obey magistrates, to be ready to every good work, to speak evil of no man, to be no brawlers, but gentle, shewing all meekness unto all men (Titus 3:1,2).

Gentleness is not weakness, but strength in restraint.

There is nothing so mighty as true gentleness, and nothing so gentle as true might.

Webster defines gentleness as free from harshness, sternness or violence. Some other names for gentleness are honorable or amiable.

In the Bible, it is listed as one of the fruits of the Holy Spirit. Unfortunately, gentleness and many of its counterparts are quickly becoming relics of the past in a society that forgets the Biblical foundation upon which it is built. How important it is for us to cultivate and nurture the growth of this priceless commodity!

David is a classic example of the true nature of God. Upon the death of his friend Jonathan, he sought after an heir, a son, anyone in his lineage to whom he could show covenant kindness—or the kindness of God. The person he found was Mephibosheth—a hopeless and helpless cripple.

As David sought after Mephibosheth, so God seeks after us. He doesn't seek to condemn us but to show us His unfailing love and kindness.

COVENANT BLESSINGS FOR THE VIRTUOUS CHRISTIAN

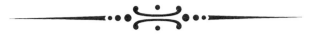

GODLINESS

I exhort therefore, that, first of all, supplications, prayers, intercessions, and giving of thanks, be made for all men; for kings, and for all that are in authority; that we may lead a quiet and peaceable life in all godliness and honesty. For this is good and acceptable in the sight of God our Saviour (1 Timothy 2:1-3).

But refuse profane and old wives' fables, and exercise thyself rather unto godliness. For bodily exercise profiteth little: but godliness is profitable unto all things, having promise of the life that now is, and of that which is to come (1 Timothy 4:7,8).

Yea, and all that will live godly in Christ Jesus shall suffer persecution (2 Timothy 3:12).

Grace and peace be multiplied unto you through the knowledge of God, and of Jesus our Lord, according as his divine power hath given unto us all things that pertain unto life and godliness, through the knowledge of him that hath called us to glory and virtue (2 Peter 1:2,3).

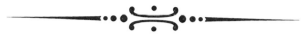

We have so lowered the standards of spiritual anointing that what we are now aiming for was once under our feet.

God does not view me as what I am today but as what I can be tomorrow.

Godliness is great gain. What is godliness? It means to be like God. If you are like God then His power will issue forth from your life.

When we begin to take a stand for godliness and righteousness, we will win America.

It is your responsibility to demonstrate godliness, no matter how frustrating a situation can be. As you display godliness, your reputation will precede you.

We are to be lights in a dark world and to exemplify the image of our heavenly Father. We cannot expect the world to come to God until first they see we have been with Him—through our outward display of His characteristics.

COVENANT BLESSINGS FOR THE VIRTUOUS CHRISTIAN

GOODNESS

The backslider in heart shall be filled with his own ways: and a good man shall be satisfied from himself (Proverb 14:14).

The evil bow before the good; and the wicked at the gates of the righteous (Proverb 14:19).

Do they not err that devise evil? but mercy and truth shall be to them that devise good (Proverb 14:22).

For ye were sometimes darkness, but now are ye light in the Lord: walk as children of light: (for the fruit of the Spirit is in all goodness and righteousness and truth); proving what is acceptable unto the Lord (Ephesians 5:8-10).

Beloved, follow not that which is evil, but that which is good. He that doeth good is of God: but he that doeth evil hath not seen God (3 John 11).

You can walk in the goodness of the Lord as long as you are anointed. As soon as you do something that grieves the Holy Spirit, however, the anointing is hindered. But don't worry because God's goodness and mercy will back you up and take care of the situation!

The world is going to come to Jesus, because they see His goodness, mercy, grace and power in us. When they see our lives, they will want to trade their lives for what we have. The goodness of God will lead the world to repentance. (Romans 2:4.)

If you want to take the limits off God in your life, become a Galatians 5 fruit-filled Christian. This includes gentleness, meekness, long-suffering, temperance, goodness, mercy and forebearing one another.

If I never saw God punish evil, I would not know He rewards goodness. If I never saw Him reward goodness, I would never know He would punish evil.

COVENANT BLESSINGS FOR THE VIRTUOUS CHRISTIAN

HOLINESS

For I am the Lord your God: ye shall therefore sanctify yourselves, and ye shall be holy; for I am holy: neither shall ye defile yourselves with any manner of creeping thing that creepeth upon the earth (Leviticus 11:44).

The fear of the Lord is the beginning of wisdom: and the knowledge of the holy is understanding (Proverb 9:10).

Having therefore these promises, dearly beloved, let us cleanse ourselves from all filthiness of the flesh and spirit, perfecting holiness in the fear of God (2 Corinthians 7:1).

And you, that were sometime alienated and enemies in your mind by wicked works, yet now hath he reconciled. In the body of his flesh through death, to present you holy and unblameable and unreproveable in his sight (Colossians 1:21,22).

Righteousness is positional and holiness is experiential. Righteousness is what God does and holiness is what we do. He deals with our character; we deal with our conduct. Righteousness gives you the power to be holy.

Holiness is not the length of your skirt or your sleeves or how you wear your hair. Holiness is separation for a specific purpose. You have been set apart by God to bring His kingdom to the earth!

It is time for the body of Christ to return to the narrow way . . . the way of holiness . . . and to become the living remnant of the Church of Jesus Christ. Only a pure and holy church, free of leaven, will ignite the smoldering embers of revival!

If you want to experience the power of God, then you will discover that it has its basis and foundation in the holiness of God. He is all powerful because He is all holy, and that separates Him from everything and anything else.

COVENANT BLESSINGS FOR THE VIRTUOUS CHRISTIAN

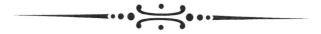

HONOR

A man's pride shall bring him low: but honour shall uphold the humble in spirit (Proverb 29:23).

For rulers are not a terror to good works, but to the evil. Wilt thou then not be afraid of the power? do that which is good, and thou shalt have praise of the same (Romans 13:3).

For this is the will of God, even your sanctification, that ye should abstain from fornication: that every one of you should know how to possess his vessel in sanctification and honour (1 Thessalonians 4:3,4).

But in a great house there are not only vessels of gold and of silver, but also of wood and of earth; and some to honour, and some to dishonour. If a man therefore purge himself from these, he shall be a vessel unto honour, sanctified, and meet for the master's use, and prepared unto every good work (2 Timothy 2:20,21).

INSPIRING INSIGHTS
by Rod Parsley

The true representation of your character is not how you respond on the mountaintop but how you respond to the raging fires and floods of life.

God is interested in people with principle who operate with character. Your character will always be your compass to keep you in line.

Honor is something that must be earned. I want to be a man of honor more than anything else. I don't ever want to bring a reproach on the kingdom of God. I want my word to be sure, straight and understood, so others may know that I live by that word.

I want God to honor my word, because I honor His Word. How can we ever expect God to honor His Word if we don't honor our own word? When you walk in honor, you have a direct link to the glory of God.

God considers you a vessel of honor. Therefore, if you are a vessel of honor, then you are fit for the Master's use.

COVENANT BLESSINGS FOR THE VIRTUOUS CHRISTIAN

HUMILITY

When men are cast down, then thou shalt say, There is lifting up; and he shall save the humble person (Job 22:29).

When he maketh inquisition for blood, he remembereth them: he forgetteth not the cry of the humble (Psalm 9:12).

The fear of the Lord is the instruction of wisdom; and before honour is humility (Proverb 15:33).

Do ye think that the scripture saith in vain, The spirit that dwelleth in us lusteth to envy? But he giveth more grace. Wherefore he saith, God resisteth the proud, but giveth grace unto the humble. Submit yourselves therefore to God. Resist the devil, and he will flee from you (James 4:5-7).

Humble yourselves in the sight of the Lord, and he shall lift you up (James 4:10).

Grace humbles us, and humility is the greatest character-building stone known in the arsenal of God. Character is the product of grace.

True humility is to realize that without Jesus, you are really insignificant in the whole scheme of His plan.

Humility is knowing who you are, who God is, and giving Him the glory for the difference.

Humility is not produced by the accolades of men nor by the badges of spiritual accomplishment. Humility is not produced in the arena of exaltation but, rather, in the arena of conflict. You are what you are in the heat of the battle!

The mountain top rarely produces humility. It is usually learned in the valley—in the midst of trial and tribulation.

There are no great men of God; there are only humble men who God chooses to greatly use.

COVENANT BLESSINGS FOR THE VIRTUOUS CHRISTIAN

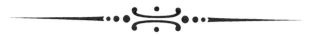

INTEGRITY

The Lord shall judge the people: judge me, O Lord, according to my righteousness, and according to mine integrity that is in me (Psalm 7:8).

Let integrity and uprightness preserve me; for I wait on thee (Psalm 25:21).

But as for me, I will walk in mine integrity: redeem me, and be merciful unto me (Psalm 26:11).

And as for me, thou upholdest me in mine integrity, and settest me before thy face for ever (Psalm 41:12).

The integrity of the upright shall guide them: but the perverseness of transgressors shall destroy them (Proverb 11:3).

The just man walketh in his integrity: his children are blessed after him (Proverb 20:7).

INSPIRING INSIGHTS
by Rod Parsley

Character is built within us, because we know who God is; therefore, we know who we are.

❖❖❖

Godly integrity is birthed out of conviction and not convenience. It does not bow at the altar of self-preservation, self-promotion or self-prominence. It does not cower to the current moral climate of the day.

Rather, integrity is the driving force behind the man or woman of God which separates them from the politically correct and socially acceptable. Allow integrity to rule your heart and guard your conduct.

❖❖❖

If you do not stand for something, you will fall for anything.

❖❖❖

As you raise the standards of spiritual intensity, moral integrity and physical purity in your personal life, the glory of God will envelope you and be a covering against the onslaught of the devil.

❖❖❖

Integrity is the whole sense of character. It is who you are when no one else is around.

COVENANT BLESSINGS FOR THE VIRTUOUS CHRISTIAN

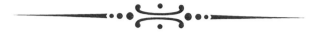

LONGSUFFERING

And ye shall be hated of all men for my name's sake. But there shall not an hair of your head perish. In your patience possess ye your souls (Luke 21:17-19).

I therefore, the prisoner of the Lord, beseech you that ye walk worthy of the vocation wherewith ye are called, with all lowliness and meekness, with longsuffering, forbearing one another in love; endeavouring to keep the unity of the Spirit in the bond of peace (Ephesians 4:1-3).

My brethren, count it all joy when ye fall into divers temptations; knowing this, that the trying of your faith worketh patience. But let patience have her perfect work, that ye may be perfect and entire, wanting nothing (James 1:2-4).

Be patient therefore, brethren, unto the coming of the Lord. Behold, the husbandman waiteth for the precious fruit of the earth, and hath long patience for it, until he receive the early and latter rain (James 5:8).

This is my definition for longsuffering . . . suffering long!

Longsuffering is given to us for one reason— to produce endurance. Endurance could be defined as the ability to remain firm in the presence of suffering and tribulation without giving into anger. Allow God to produce the fruit of longsuffering in your life, so you may be able to endure the onslaught of Satan!

If you're going to make it, God is going to produce the fruit of longsuffering in your life. Then every time temptation and distress come your way, you will march over these alien armies and trample them under your feet!

Have you ever noticed all the places you have an opportunity to exercise longsuffering? Places like the fast food drive-through window or rush hour traffic at 5:00 p.m. are prime opportunities to cultivate the fruit of longsuffering. When you have longsuffering produced in your life, you will remain steadfast.

COVENANT BLESSINGS FOR THE VIRTUOUS CHRISTIAN

MOTIVES

And thou, Solomon my son, know thou the God of thy father, and serve him with a perfect heart and with a willing mind: for the Lord searcheth all hearts, and understandeth all the imaginations of the thoughts: if thou seek him, he will be found of thee; but if thou forsake him, he will cast thee off for ever (1 Chronicles 28:9).

I will behave myself wisely in a perfect way. O when wilt thou come unto me? I will walk within my house with a perfect heart (Psalm 101:2).

Search me, O God, and know my heart: try me, and know my thoughts: and see if there be any wicked way in me, and lead me in the way everlasting (Psalm 139:23,24).

The thoughts of the righteous are right: but the counsels of the wicked are deceit (Proverb 12:5).

It is not what we wear on the outside that matters but what burns in the sanctuary of our hearts.

Always be sure your motives are pure. It doesn't matter if your actions are seen by someone. The important thing is to touch a person's life everyday. Perhaps you just make someone feel better by offering an encouraging word, but do it out of a heart full of the love of Jesus.

❖❖❖

The world bases success on the manipulation of personality ethics—doing the right things without the right motives.

❖❖❖

God is interested in people with biblical, moral and ethical values whom He can trust to operate within those character building ethics.

There is a big difference between character and reputation. Reputation is what people think about you, but character is what God knows about you.

COVENANT BLESSINGS FOR THE VIRTUOUS CHRISTIAN

PURITY OF HEART

Who shall ascend into the hill of the Lord? or who shall stand in his holy place? He that hath clean hands, and a pure heart; who hath not lifted up his soul unto vanity, nor sworn deceitfully. He shall receive the blessing from the Lord, and righteousness from the God of his salvation (Psalm 24:3-5).

Blessed are the pure in heart: for they shall see God (Matthew 5:8).

Pure religion and undefiled before God and the Father is this, to visit the fatherless and widows in their affliction, and to keep himself unspotted from the world (James 1:27).

Seeing ye have purified your souls in obeying the truth through the Spirit unto unfeigned love of the brethren, see that ye love one another with a pure heart fervently: being born again, not of corruptible seed, but of incorruptible, by the word of God, which liveth and abideth for ever (1 Peter 1:22,23).

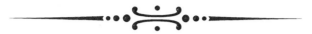

God is not concerned with anything except that you obey Him. So many times we focus on our works for Him. We say, "Look what I did here. I've said the right 72 confessions. I go to church 3 times a week." That is works.

It's only when your service comes out of a pure motive and a pure heart of love toward God He will then begin to flow in your life.

The major thing that makes people live right is to realize they are serving a holy God. He is a fire from His loins up and a fire from His loins down. He has given us the ability to walk in purity and holiness for Him; and He makes us stronger than every temptation.

Purity in private brings power in public. Purity will only come through your relationship with Jesus Christ, through reading His Word and through praying every day. Then the sins that try to attack your life will fall before they ever touch you, by the anointing of God which comes forth from your life.

COVENANT BLESSINGS FOR THE VIRTUOUS CHRISTIAN

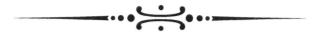

RIGHTEOUSNESS

Cast thy burden upon the Lord, and he shall sustain thee: he shall never suffer the righteous to be moved (Psalm 55:22).

Say ye to the righteous, that it shall be well with him: for they shall eat the fruit of their doings (Isaiah 3:10).

Blessed are they which do hunger and thirst after righteousness: for they shall be filled (Matthew 5:6).

For he hath made him to be sin for us, who knew no sin; that we might be made the righteousness of God in him (2 Corinthians 5:21).

For the eyes of the Lord are over the righteous, and his ears are open unto their prayers: but the face of the Lord is against them that do evil (1 Peter 3:12).

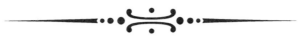

In order to have an impact on our society, God is moving the body of Christ to rise far above the status quo of church as normal. We live in a society where right has been wrong for so long that righteousness has become abnormal.

Righteousness does not overlook sin; it overcomes it!

If you will become established in righteousness, regardless of when you fall from God's grace, righteousness will re-establish you and keep the devil from constantly condemning you.

Righteousness doesn't keep you from sinning. Rather, it gives you the opportunity to overcome sin and the power to resist it. How good it feels when temptation knocks at the door and righteousness answers!

Temptation will tuck its tail and run away. As you stand behind the door and watch it go, the Holy Ghost pats you on the back like you did the whole thing yourself—even though it was He who gave you power beyond your own power! Blessed be the name of the Lord!

COVENANT BLESSINGS FOR THE VIRTUOUS CHRISTIAN

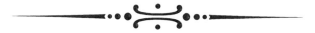

TEMPERANCE

Know ye not that they which run in a race run all, but one receiveth the prize? So run, that ye may obtain. And every man that striveth for the mastery is temperate in all things. Now they do it to obtain a corruptible crown; but we an incorruptible. I therefore so run, not as uncertainly; so fight I, not as one that beateth the air: But I keep under my body, and bring it into subjection: lest that by any means, when I have preached to others, I myself should be a castaway (1 Corinthians 9:24-27).

Let your moderation be known unto all men. The Lord is at hand (Philippians 4:5).

And beside this, giving all diligence, add to your faith virtue; and to virtue knowledge; and to knowledge temperance; and to temperance patience; and to patience godliness; and to godliness brotherly kindness; and to brotherly kindness charity. For if these things be in you, and abound, they make you that ye shall neither be barren nor unfruitful in the knowledge of our Lord Jesus Christ (2 Peter 1:5-8).

INSPIRING INSIGHTS
by Rod Parsley

Temperance is the ability to exercise self-control and moderation in every situation. It is a fruit of the Spirit which God wants us to develop in our everyday life.

God wants you to learn to live a fasted life. This means to do without some things that you don't need. Deny your flesh some things.

Our problem in America is we want everything, and we want it right now. We must learn to live a life of temperance and self-control.

Learn to live a life of discipline. Anything you can't live without you don't need.

We need a life and emotions that are controlled and not controlling. We need to learn to practice temperance.

It is time for you to take your rightful place of dominion on the face of the earth and declare the decree of the Lord. Speak the law of the Lord, and control the atmosphere of your life.

ROD PARSLEY CELEBRATING
REPAIRING THE BREACH • RAISING THE STANDARD
• REAPING THE HARVEST •

20th ANNIVERSARY

COVENANT
BLESSINGS
of
Heaven

COVENANT BLESSINGS
OF HEAVEN

BLESSED HOPE

Behold, I shew you a mystery; we shall not all sleep, but we shall all be changed, in a moment, in the twinkling of an eye, at the last trump: for the trumpet shall sound, and the dead shall be raised incorruptible, and we shall be changed (1 Corinthians 15:51,52).

For the Lord himself shall descend from heaven with a shout, with the voice of the archangel, and with the trump of God: and the dead in Christ shall rise first: then we which are alive and remain shall be caught up together with them in the clouds, to meet the Lord in the air: and so shall we ever be with the Lord. Wherefore comfort one another with these words (1 Thessalonians 4:16-18).

For the grace of God that bringeth salvation hath appeared to all men, teaching us that, denying ungodliness and worldly lusts, we should live soberly, righteously, and godly, in this present world; looking for that blessed hope, and the glorious appearing of the great God and our Saviour Jesus Christ (Titus 2:11-13).

INSPIRING INSIGHTS
by Rod Parsley

In the twinkling of an eye, gravity is going to lose its hold, and you are going to leave this planet! This world is not your home! You are just a sojourner (temporary resident) here! You are getting ready to take an extraterrestrial trip!

Those chariots that haven't ridden the wind since Elijah are getting ready to be pulled out of their stalls and strapped to steaming white stallions. The Son of God is getting ready to slide His long, lean Galilean leg into the stirrup of a steaming white stallion. The crash of His great whip is going to billow out across the expanse of time and space like the crash of a thousand cannons. Jesus is coming back for you and me!

❖❖❖

I have been watching and waiting for the Eastern sky to be peeled back like an orange since the time I came to Jesus Christ. The Bible has not changed. Jesus is coming again!

The resurrection of all who have fallen asleep in Christ . . . and their translation together with those who are alive and remain unto the coming of the Lord . . . is our imminent and blessed hope.

20*th* ANNIVERSARY

COVENANT BLESSINGS
OF HEAVEN

ETERNAL JOY

Thou wilt shew me the path of life: in thy presence is fulness of joy; at thy right hand there are pleasures for evermore (Psalm 16:11).

Therefore the redeemed of the Lord shall return, and come with singing unto Zion; and everlasting joy shall be upon their head: they shall obtain gladness and joy; and sorrow and mourning shall flee away (Isaiah 51:11).

Whom having not seen, ye love; in whom, though now ye see him not, yet believing, ye rejoice with joy unspeakable and full of glory: receiving the end of your faith, even the salvation of your souls (1 Peter 1:8,9).

Now unto him that is able to keep you from falling, and to present you faultless before the presence of his glory with exceeding joy, to the only wise God our Saviour, be glory and majesty, dominion and power, both now and ever. Amen (Jude 24,25).

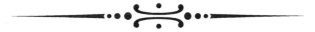

Joy is something that is rooted deeper than happiness. I'm talking about joy in the morning; joy at midnight; joy at noon; joy when the doctor looks at you and says you have to die and cannot live; and joy when your kids are on drugs.

You will have joy when they say all manner of evil against you falsely; joy when you don't have a dollar to change; joy when you don't know who your friends are. I'm not talking about something you have to work up. I'm talking about something you can't shut down. Joy!

❖❖❖

You can have a deep-rooted, Rock of Gibraltar, in-the-middle-of-trouble joy! When your heart is breaking, the world is dying and the moon is bleeding, you can have joy, unspeakable and full of glory! (1 Peter 1:8.)

The seedbed of joy is obedience.

Joy is a force just as faith is a force. In your darkest hour of tribulation, it will be your strength to guide you through every line of Satan's defense!

COVENANT BLESSINGS
OF HEAVEN

ETERNAL LIFE

And Jesus answered and said, Verily I say unto you, There is no man that hath left house, or brethren, or sisters, or father, or mother, or wife, or children, or lands, for my sake, and the gospel's, but he shall receive an hundredfold now in this time, houses, and brethren, and sisters, and mothers, and children, and lands, with persecutions; and in the world to come eternal life (Mark 10:29,30).

But after that the kindness and love of God our Saviour toward man appeared, not by works of righteousness which we have done, but according to his mercy he saved us, by the washing of regeneration, and renewing of the Holy Ghost; which he shed on us abundantly through Jesus Christ our Saviour; that being justified by his grace, we should be made heirs according to the hope of eternal life (Titus 3:4-7).

Keep yourselves in the love of God, looking for the mercy of our Lord Jesus Christ unto eternal life (Jude 21).

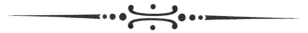

The day you were born again, God reached into His heart and pulled out eternal life. Eternal . . . it's a thought that our finite minds cannot even grasp. Eternal life is a gift.

We serve some kind of God! What in the world would He withhold from you? Healing? Deliverance? He gave you eternal life! You are an eternal, spirit being who will never cease to exist! Just think of what He has in store for you because the Bible says, "But as it is written, Eye hath not seen, nor ear heard, neither have entered into the heart of man, the things which God hath prepared for them that love him" (1 Corinthians 2:9).

The free gift of God is eternal life. Eternal life—sufficient in quantity, superior in quality!

One day, because of the cross of Jesus Christ, God will wipe away all tears from your eyes. You will have eternal life in heaven where we'll sorrow no more, we'll be sick no more and we'll be hungry no more! There are no houses made of cardboard in heaven. There are no children who don't have enough to eat in heaven. There are no more wars in heaven. Your Bible says the former things will pass away and God will make all things new!

COVENANT BLESSINGS
OF HEAVEN

ETERNAL PEACE

And they brought him to Jesus: and they cast their garments upon the colt, and they set Jesus thereon. And as he went, they spread their clothes in the way. And when he was come nigh, even now at the descent of the mount of Olives, the whole multitude of the disciples began to rejoice and praise God with a loud voice for all the mighty works that they had seen; saying, Blessed be the King that cometh in the name of the Lord: peace in heaven, and glory in the highest (Luke 19:35-38).

For the kingdom of God is not meat and drink; but righteousness, and peace, and joy in the Holy Ghost (Romans 14:17).

Looking for and hasting unto the coming of the day of God, wherein the heavens being on fire shall be dissolved, and the elements shall melt with fervent heat? Nevertheless we, according to his promise, look for new heavens and a new earth, wherein dwelleth righteousness. Wherefore, beloved, seeing that ye look for such things, be diligent that ye may be found of him in peace, without spot, and blameless (2 Peter 3:12-14).

The Lord wants to infuse you with something so powerful that it will be forever indelibly marked upon your remembrance—peace. Let it fly as a flag over your life and a memorial before God. Then when striving begins to start, peace will come.

Jeremiah 29:11 says, "For I know the thoughts that I think toward you, saith the Lord, thoughts of peace, and not of evil, to give you an expected end." Another translation says God has plans for your welfare and not for calamity.

You have a future in this kingdom. There may be calamity in your life, but it is not the plan of God for you. His kingdom is a kingdom of peace and of hope.

God wants to give you eternal peace borne out of a life in right standing with Him. It is a peace that in the moment of your life's greatest tragedy, you can lift your hands and, with tears streaming down your face, you can say, "I have absolute peace with God, and there is nothing between me and Jesus."

COVENANT BLESSINGS OF HEAVEN

ETERNAL REST

And it shall come to pass in the day that the Lord shall give thee rest from thy sorrow, and from thy fear, and from the hard bondage wherein thou wast made to serve (Isaiah 14:3).

Come unto me, all ye that labour and are heavy laden, and I will give you rest. Take my yoke upon you, and learn of me; for I am meek and lowly in heart: and ye shall find rest unto your souls. (Matthew 11:28,29).

There remaineth therefore a rest to the people of God. For he that is entered into his rest, he also hath ceased from his own works, as God did from his. Let us labour therefore to enter into that rest, lest any man fall after the same example of unbelief (Hebrews 4:9-11).

And I heard a voice from heaven saying unto me, Write, Blessed are the dead which die in the Lord from henceforth: yea, saith the Spirit, that they may rest from their labours; and their works do follow them (Revelation 14:13).

In the Old Testament you couldn't get close to God or understand Him. But in John chapter 1, you find Him wrapped in swaddling clothes, with angels singing happy birthday and heralding the name of Jesus.

This is the name the God-man carried as a young boy in the Jewish synagogue. He carried it through His earthly ministry. He carried that name to an old rugged cross, and the Father said, "There hangs the gift of my salvation."

Could Jesus really break the penalty of sin and bring us into eternal rest and allow us to fulfill the purpose for which you and I were created upon this earth? He can and He did! He has made a way for us to rest from the labor and toil of sin!

As you experience the revelation of who Jesus is, the love which He manifests toward you, and the care and attention which He gives to His children, then you will know Him in a brand new dimension. You will be able to rest in His hands in a way you never thought possible.

COVENANT BLESSINGS
OF HEAVEN

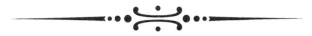

ETERNAL REUNION

Let not your heart be troubled: ye believe in God, believe also in me. In my Father's house are many mansions: if it were not so, I would have told you. I go to prepare a place for you. And if I go and prepare a place for you, I will come again, and receive you unto myself; that where I am, there ye may be also (John 14:1-3).

For now we see through a glass, darkly; but then face to face: now I know in part; but then shall I know even as also I am known (1 Corinthians 13:12).

Who shall change our vile body, that it may be fashioned like unto his glorious body, according to the working whereby he is able even to subdue all things unto himself (Philippians 3:21).

And I heard a great voice out of heaven saying, Behold, the tabernacle of God is with men, and he will dwell with them, and they shall be his people, and God himself shall be with them, and be their God (Revelation 21:3).

INSPIRING INSIGHTS
by Rod Parsley

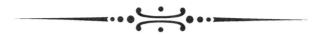

Heaven is a place of reunion. We are going to see loved ones who have gone before us: Peter, John the Beloved, Paul the apostle and Elijah, just to name a few, will all be there. My grandmother will be there. My uncle who went to be with the Lord from a rice paddy in Vietnam, in 1969, will be there. Dr. Sumrall and Smith Wigglesworth will be there. All who have gone before us will be waiting for us to cross the threshold into the gates of that great city. There will be no more tears of loneliness for we will see them again.

❖❖❖

I would venture to say you have someone waiting just over on the glory side. I believe Ira Stamphill said it best, "I have a mansion just over the hillside in that bright land where we will never grow old. And, someday yonder we will never more wander, but walk on streets that are made of gold."

But the greatest homecoming will be when I see Jesus. For 10,000 times 10,000 years I will bathe His precious, nail-pierced feet with tears of gratitude for all that He has done for me. Even now I love to sing, "Oh, I want to see Him, look upon His face, there to sing forever of His saving grace. On the streets of glory let me lift my voice, cares all past, home at last, ever to rejoice!"

COVENANT BLESSINGS OF HEAVEN

ETERNAL REWARD

For what is our hope, or joy, or crown of rejoicing? Are not even ye in the presence of our Lord Jesus Christ at his coming? For ye are our glory and joy (1 Thessalonians 2:19, 20).

I have fought a good fight, I have finished my course, I have kept the faith: henceforth there is laid up for me a crown of righteousness, which the Lord, the righteous judge, shall give me at that day: and not to me only, but unto all them also that love his appearing (2 Timothy 4:7,8).

And when the chief Shepherd shall appear, ye shall receive a crown of glory that fadeth not away (1 Peter 5:4).

Fear none of those things which thou shalt suffer: behold, the devil shall cast some of you into prison, that ye may be tried; and ye shall have tribulation ten days: be thou faithful unto death, and I will give thee a crown of life (Revelation 2:10).

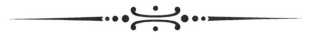

There is a crown of rejoicing for the soul winner. There is a crown of righteousness for those who love His appearance. There is a crown of life for the persecuted Christian. And there is a crown of victory for the overcomer. The prize of your endurance will be the words spoken by Jesus on that grand and glorious day, "Well done good and faithful servant . . . enter thou into the joy of thy Lord" (Matthew 25:23).

God is a rewarder, and He promises you an eternal reward for the sacrifices you have made.

There are some crowns waiting for you in heaven, and I want to receive a collection of them. Because when I get to the end, through David's tabernacle and down Hallelujah Boulevard, past the trees with the leaves for the healing of the nations; when I wade through the River of Life at the end there's a throne. When I get there I want to have some crowns to cast down at Jesus' feet!

COVENANT BLESSINGS OF HEAVEN

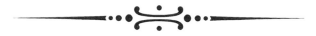

HEAVEN

He stretcheth out the north over the empty place, and hangeth the earth upon nothing (Job 26:7).

Beautiful for situation, the joy of the whole earth, is mount Zion, on the sides of the north, the city of the great King. God is known in her palaces for a refuge (Psalm 48:2,3).

Blessed be the God and Father of our Lord Jesus Christ, which according to his abundant mercy hath begotten us again unto a lively hope by the resurrection of Jesus Christ from the dead, to an inheritance incorruptible, and undefiled, and that fadeth not away, reserved in heaven for you (1 Peter 1:3,4).

And I saw a new heaven and a new earth: for the first heaven and the first earth were passed away; and there was no more sea. And I John saw the holy city, new Jerusalem, coming down from God out of heaven, prepared as a bride adorned for her husband (Revelation 21:1,2).

It would not really matter to me if the gates of heaven were made of wood or if they swung on leather hinges. It would not matter to me if there was mud in the streets knee-deep, and the mansions were nothing but cardboard shanties. Because, when I look at the end of that muddy street, at the end of that heavenly boulevard, I will see Jesus, my everlasting Savior and Friend.

In heaven there will not be any need for the sun nor the moon. We are going to a land where there will not be any darkness. There will be no more pain or sorrow. There will be no more death and no obituary pages in the Heavenly Gazette. There will be no doctors' offices, no sanitariums, and there will be no more devil!

I can only imagine that heaven is a vast museum of Jesus' grace and mercy. I believe it is a mansion of miracles and a place in which everything will astonish each of its new citizens.

Dwight L. Moody caught a glimpse of the glory awaiting the blood-washed saints before he went on to be with the Lord. He said, "Earth recedes and heaven opens before me. If this is death, it is sweet." I cannot wait to go there!

About the Author

Rod Parsley began his ministry as an energetic seventeen-year-old in the backyard of his parents' Ohio home. The fresh, "old-time gospel" approach of Parsley's delivery immediately attracted a hungry, God-seeking audience. From the 17 people who attended Parsley's first 1977 backyard meeting, the crowds rapidly grew.

Today, as the pastor of Columbus, Ohio's 5200-seat World Harvest Church, Parsley oversees World Harvest Christian Academy; World Harvest Bible College; Bridge of Hope missions and outreach; and "Breakthrough," World Harvest Church's daily and weekly television broadcast.

Parsley's message to "Raise the Standards" of spiritual intensity, moral integrity and physical purity not only extends across North America, but also spans the globe to 136 nations via television and shortwave radio.

Thousands in arenas across the country and around the world experience the saving, healing, delivering message of Jesus Christ as Parsley calls people back to Bible basics.

Rod Parsley currently resides in Pickerington, Ohio, with his wife, Joni, and their two children, Ashton and Austin.

Notes

Notes

Notes

ROD PARSLEY CELEBRATING
REPAIRING THE BREACH • RAISING THE STANDARD
• REAPING THE HARVEST •
20th ANNIVERSARY